THE DYNAMIC WAY
OF MEDITATION

A description of how Vipassana meditation
can liberate the true self from inherited
pain and conditioning.

Dear Gene —
 It has been good. God
be with you as you grow
in truth.
 I will see you often —
 A Friend
 Bob.

By the same author
THE WAY OF NON-ATTACHMENT

THE DYNAMIC WAY OF MEDITATION

The Release and Cure of Pain and Suffering

by

DHIRAVAMSA

Foreword by Claudio Naranjo

TURNSTONE PRESS LIMITED
Wellingborough, Northamptonshire

First published 1982

British Library Cataloguing in Publication Data

Dhiravamsa
    The dynamic way of meditation: the release and cure
    of pain and suffering.
    1. Vipásyaná (Buddhism)
    I. Title
    294.3'443   BQ5630.V5

    ISBN 0-85500-163-1

Photoset by Glebe Graphics, Wilby, Northamptonshire,
printed in Great Britain by Nene Litho,
Earls Barton, Northamptonshire
and bound by Woolnough Bookbinding,
Wellingborough, Northamptonshire.

CONTENTS

FOREWORD

Born in Thailand and trained as a monk, Dhiravamsa is probably one of the most creative representatives of Theravada Buddhism in the West.

Western beginners and even advanced practitioners of Eastern approaches often run the risk of becoming – as a consequence of their reverence toward traditions to which they are relatively new – a little literal, if not imitative. And even experienced Easterners, out of an ingrained adherence to traditions, may attain mastery of what they were taught but show little inclination towards cultural or technical exploration and integration.

Dhiravamsa, however, is an exception. Solidly grounded in his oriental apprenticeship of meditation and abhidharma, he feels little inclined towards repetition, but improvises in his talks in a style that reflects both his personal experience and his continuing adventure in the teaching process.

Dhiravamsa's most striking contribution to the practice of meditation is his work in the interphase between classical Vipassana and expression: the spontaneous expression that is likely to occur after sufficient sitting and attention, if it is only allowed, and of which he talks as a healing release.

It is not that spontaneous expression has not been observed in classical Theravada experience. The case is, rather, that little has been said about it, and that, traditionally, it has only been allowed, but not invited. Even less invited is it in Zen Buddhism, where expressive phenomena – whether motor, affective, or visionary (and these may be regarded as internalized expression) – are carefully avoided distractions. This is surely a valid strategy – as the Zen tradition shows – but we can also say that the opposite is equally valid: spontaneous expression constitutes the process that Indian Tantrism conceptualizes as the awakening of the *kundalini* – a dormant spiritual power in the body – and which it welcomes as a process of purification. This is just what Dhiravamsa advises his students to do.

In my own judgement both the inhibition of impulses and their expression can serve awareness training – and each, by itself, has its drawbacks: inhibition involves the danger of repression; expression, that of ego-involvement. Thus, for over a decade I have been espousing the view that both should be cultivated side by side, not only in meditation, but in psychotherapy, and in life – and for this I have naturally received the criticism of single-technique oriented practitioners. I feel refreshed that somebody with the traditional background and the spiritual stature of Dhiravamsa has arrived, in his own style, to the same basic formula. And I feel even more refreshed by his implicit but clear recognition of expression as a constitutive element of meditation, because I believe that it is important not only to acknowledge the validity of expression as a path, but to understand that the expressive element (in a broad sense of the term, including the mobilization of 'meditative energy' and the phenomena today termed 'unstressing') is a component of all meditation, just like calm and clarity. For meditation involves not only one-sided control, (beyond elementary levels) but freedom, and not pure quiescence, but life.

What Dhiravamsa teaches agrees with my experience, and with the best that I have learnt, first in Gestalt Therapy, then in

Tibetan Buddhism: the fusion of awareness and spontaneity.

Claudio Naranjo
Leksand, Sweden

1.

RELEASE AND CURE

Our human condition reveals to us time and time again that we must constantly deal with emotional and psychological strain, stress and tension as well as physical pain, suffering and illness. What we seek is a remedy, or methods, by which our problems and difficulties may be resolved. In other words, we want to be free from our condition.

This is all very obvious to us existing in this modern world. Due to the continually increasing demand for release and cure, we find that the supply of therapeutic techniques and various forms of treatment is also on the increase. On the traditional level, society provides medical doctors, psychiatrists, psychologists, psychotherapists and priests. At the same time, many individuals render their services in the form of teachers, healers, clairvoyants, astrologers, and so on.

Those who feel that they need help in these stressful times can quite easily find methods of treatment ranging from gurus and shamans to institutional therapy. It is interesting to see how we have come to respond to our personal situations, to our difficulties and challenges, and those of others, by this quest for release and cure.

What is emerging is that illnesses, conflict, and pain involve the totality of human growth and development as well as an awakening from our psychological sleep and ignorance – the absence of awareness of reality. What people involved in this search are discovering is that without those disturbing factors, either at the personal or interpersonal level, such as marriage or partnership, or on the level of general human relationships, we can never grow into full humanness, and reach the beyond.

If we maintain a realistic view of life and all the situations it presents to us, we can take the drama and the dilemma that we encounter as a challenge for bringing out and making use of our inner resources, our human capacities and potentialities; in other words, we can allow the seeds of our humanity to grow out of the experience and wholeness of being to reveal itself and to merge with all circumstances related to existence in this constantly changing world.

In this way we can begin to learn how to cope with ourselves and to curb our difficulties constructively and creatively so as to be able to let go of that which hinders our growth and maturation, the natural flow of life and the unfolding of our real being. Instead of being victimized in the face of negative or destructive experiences or unexpected or unavoidable illness, we come fully to accept facts and reality with understanding and patience. This is the means whereby we clear away the barriers that prevent us from experiencing well-being. We shall then be able to clean out or release all unhealthy, impure and locked-in energies within our bodies and minds, and to flow naturally with strength and health.

In the final analysis, we ourselves are the vehicles by which liberation is achieved. We merely have to witness and provide hospitality for the remedy and the discharge, the release and cure. With this as the guiding light within us, we shall steadily move forward toward a fullness of being, until it is completely in charge of our life. This is the end of Dukkha (the pleasure/pain principle) as stated by Gotama the Buddha. This is living Nirvana, the total extinction of fire and smoke.

If we look into our life situations, we will realize that there are many types of fires burning inside the psychosomatic structures known as mind and body. Under the influence of fires of compulsive desire, hatred, delusion, envy, jealousy, pride, ambition, uncertainty, fear and so forth, we are ablaze. We burn all day long and send out smoke by night. This is common to all humans, and leads to incessant creation and accumulation of all sorts of activities such as habits, fixed models of reaction, inflexibility, conflicts, constrictions, contraction and expansion through excessively reactive behaviour. Creative as well as destructive actions are performed for one's own benefit and for the welfare or disaster of others, either consciously or unconsciously.

Now the point is that whatever we do both to ourselves and to others becomes deposited as conditioning within our personality, a unit of ego-self, so to speak. And this deposited conditioning will be deepened and strengthened through the different games that we play with ourselves and in relating with others. Feeling disturbed, uncomfortable, nervous and uneasy but not knowing precisely what is going on, we look for compensation to cover up the real issue by turning away from the actual and obvious situation, and getting involved in activities disassociated with it. This is how human neuroses expand, renew and prolong themselves. We keep drugging ourselves so that we will not feel the pain, and the result is that we become numb and sleepy, insensitive and deaf in our existence.

For example, some people are unable to listen to that which threatens their belief, tradition or way of thinking: because it is painful they turn it into something ridiculous or illogical. Others simply become deaf to the message that is frightening or disturbing, or that uncovers their original pain, which is to be protected at all costs by the ego-defence mechanism ('I don't want to hear it!').

But by turning towards ourselves and by continuing to return to the present and the obvious, we can sit, walk, stand, move and be with that which is actually within us and around us. In doing this we will get to know all our inner and outer situations and occurrences accurately, which means that our actions, reactions and responses are clearly seen and watched constantly without our imposing any ideas or ideals on them. The flame of watching will take full charge of burning and eliminating the undesirable, destructive and unhealthy factors of life. This is natural and spontaneous.

What is needed for this work is the trusting willingness to throw ourselves into the flame of attention, the act of simply but intensely attending to whatever arises in any moment with no idea of doing anything in particular or becoming anybody special. Then see what happens. It is by accepting ourselves as we are and recognizing facts and realities that we naturally reduce our resistances and open the doors for honest communication and sympathetic understanding to take place, without creating any distortion of reality; in this way no further conflict will be encouraged. At this point, the act of releasing begins to operate with a surge of creative energy.

For the past nine years, since 1973, I have been learning a great deal, from those participating with me in retreats, about the expression of physical and psychic energies in different forms. This occurs mainly during the sitting meditation, and then carries over into the walking, standing and reclining meditation until the release is completed. These expressions include twitching, shaking, stretching in various positions, sometimes entering into very difficult yoga-type postures hitherto unknown to the meditator and rolling on the floor or the ground. Sometimes sounds arise, such as heavy breathing, crying, weeping, sudden screams, laughter and angry words. Body expression includes movement of hands which may hit or hammer specific parts of the body such as the knees and thighs, or the floor and cushions placed in front of the meditator; at times the hands will move to massage the belly or pelvic region, the legs, knees, solar plexus and chest. Expression is also experienced in the face and head; the neck may stretch and rotate, as well as the eyes, while the mouth and jaw open widely and sometimes suddenly, accompanied by sound.

Each form of expression is the release of negative states of emotion and psychological conditioning kept or retained in particular points and regions of the body as well as in the psyche. This means that the individual meditator relives the past experiences and karma accumulated mainly in early life through unhealthy and destructive relationships with parents and those close to him. Also, the reliving of negative feelings such as anger, hatred, resentment, hostility, shame, hurt, frustration and fear stored up through relationships with a lover, partner or boss can be strongly felt by those who have carried along with them such repressed feelings.

Recently, we have found that more and more meditators have got in touch with their birth experience, reliving and releasing the traumatic pain involved, and seeing the fear, anger, frustration and confusion at the actual time of being born. In this connection the Buddha stated, 'Painful indeed is being born again and again'. The pain and suffering from birth in this lifetime is quite unbearable for many of us and leads to tremendous problems in our psychological and emotional existence which we find not easy to resolve. How much more so if we add the birth traumas of other lifetimes too.

Some meditators complain that the process of release and cure and the clearing away of karma seems never to end. It goes on and on, often more intensely as time passes. What is the answer? Only patience, understanding and learning to live , with such work in trust and with alert awareness will give them the true answer. For everyone is suffering. Some do so quietly and others are noisy. Suffering is just a part of the life experience through which we come to know the facts and reality related to our lives both individually and collectively.

At this point I would like to clarify the matter of release or expression in meditation, particularly for the sake of those of you who have been undergoing the process and who feel discouraged or impatient.

There are many different layers of tension, pain and suffering in the body which provide containers for negative energies and repressed feelings. If they remain unseen these can acquire explosive power. This comes about through the contraction of muscles when reactive feelings arise as habitual and automatic responses to sense experiences, including those of the mental world. At each point of contact, through the eyes, ears, nose, mouth, touch or mind, there arises a sensation or feeling which immediately associates itself with certain ideas or impulses so as to produce an obvious reaction either internally or externally. Each reaction, in the body or the mind, causes muscular contraction. At that moment the container, so to speak, is provided and the negative feeling is stored up. Then the unexpressed feelings supported by fear build up the pattern of reacting; and these reactive behaviour patterns become automatic, habitual, unconscious (certainly at the moment of reacting) and uncontrollable; i.e. you do not want to react in a certain way, but do so anyway. Each time you react you deepen the pattern and therefore it gets stronger and becomes more powerful. It then takes full command over you. At this stage you are no longer 'yourself', because the layers of karma are concentrated into various contracted parts of the body. Some layers contain more tension, more pain and more suffering than others, particularly the ones on the periphery. The deeper you go, the more painful it becomes, until the final release is obtained.

If you expect quick relief, you become impatient, and you may begin to react negatively to the whole unpredictable process. This will add more karma to that already existing. And so the cycle goes on. Samsara continues its process through passion, action and reaction.

I would also like to make clear how the process of release and cure becomes complicated. This happens because of two main factors: the interference of ego, and the weakness of awareness.

When the ego begins to realize that the body has the power to express itself more freely, removing its blockages and letting vital liberating energy flow, it gets frightened of losing control over the body and all the containers, because this means the destruction of the ego's own energy sources, which it has built up for its own survival. So it steps up its control over all the expressions, using the body as a tool for deluding and deceiving the expressive meditators, making them feel good, or psychologically free for a while, or excited. In this way meditators undergoing the process become performers.

Often this is not very obvious to the meditator because his mind concentrates on cleaning up every negativity completely, and on freeing the body of all the locked energies. So the intention behind the performance has some validity. But it still remains an ego game. This weakening of awareness stems from the fact that the meditator is not observing the actual event clearly, for the excitement and anticipation of the goal has become much more attractive than seeing and penetrating into the process itself.

When awareness is keen, the meditator may become blinded, made deaf and insensitive to his situation. Without looking, seeing cannot take place, and without seeing, there can be no liberation. Without total liberation, the cure does not come to fruition; instead of release, a sort of leaking takes place, providing a slight but temporary relief. With some frustration, meditators at this point may begin to react against the process, bringing more pain and suffering into their lives.

The effective way is found when the meditator becomes neutral and inwardly silent in relation to what is happening; when he remains still in any movement or posture that arises. Control is not required. Let go of everything and allow anything to happen of its own accord. Just breathe and watch and patiently live through what is going on with intelligence. Any attempt to obstruct or postpone the work merely results in pain and violence as the energy of release gathers momentum. Let the whole body and mind be worked on completely. Then everything will be taken care of. Your non-interfering awareness is constantly applied and you are fully in touch with what is going on, so that you never miss the opportunity to see clearly what it is all about, and what lies beyond what you are experiencing. With such simple, clear awareness, you remain alert and fully awake, ready to perceive any signals and move on freely.

Those who become attached to the negative find it hard to appreciate a good positive feeling. The denial of the reality of the positive side deepens the identification with the negativity. Then the only things that appear real are the negative, while good feelings seem unreal, or too good to-be real. This is how reality becomes distorted. But with an open attitude, we can allow both sides of experience to come through without favouring one and rejecting the other. We have to come to regard all experiences, good and bad, as equal, and move towards equanimity concerning the conflicting conditioned states, harmonizing the opposites and rising above conflict and paradoxes.

Instead of being tied down to lower states we will then be lifted up to dance with the higher reality, while remaining aware of the unpleasant sensations left over from the experience of the lower world.

Although expression in meditation is the natural means of cleansing the karmic accumulations, particularly at the psychological and emotional levels of existence, we still need to examine the nature of expression thoroughly so that we will not take it for granted.

Through 'expression' in meditation we spontaneously reveal our real selves and release our inhibitions of personality. This is an individual psychological revolution for we permit ourselves to be authentic and act from our own centres, not from any source of cultural, religious or parental authority. Having our experiences clarified in a group, or with somebody related to the incident (or privately, if meditating alone), will help to purify our emotions and release blockages in the body and the mind.

But we must be very clear that expression is different from reaction. The latter is doing something to someone that has hurt or upset you with the desire to crush and destroy them either physically or verbally; but the former focuses attention on the state of emotion or feeling itself for the sole purpose of being rid of it, or letting it melt, but not giving it to anyone. This may be done with or without a witness.

Another form of expression comes out in the form of explosion as will be described in detail in the next chapter. Real expression leads to the ending of karma, but reaction accumulates more karma and deepens the reactive patterns of behaviour. And because expression could turn into a reaction and game playing in a subtle way, I would therefore like to take this opportunity to warn all expressive meditators of some side-effects of expression. Here are some observations: First, gentle or violent repetitious expression with a little release indicates the interference of ego and mere excitement of the body due to the lack of sensitive awareness. If this happens, watch and look into such expressions deeply and carefully. Do not encourage them to continue. When keeping them in close check, you will gain clear insight into the whole situation and get on with the work without wasting your time and energy, and you will avoid complications.

Secondly, the motivation and self-programming for releasing and expressing, or for cleaning out your psycho-physical system, is not real expression and does not help to increase awareness but merely promotes ego trips. Always remember that expressions without awareness may produce some relief but not the cure, the simple reason being that they are the acts of a performer who is motivated by the desire to please himself or others, so that the major amount of energy is directed at release over and over again, with little left for cultivating and nurturing the seed of insight. So growth cannot take place when the production of creative energy is not in the right proportion to the energy released. And when clear awareness is not present, the excessive energy released will be conducive to mental instability.

Therefore, bear in mind that awareness and insight play a very essential part in the process of release and cure. With awareness you are safeguarded; without it you could be in danger. So when employing the various techniques, or when doing exercises for eliminating unhealthy energies, make sure that awareness is present, and let it flow in and out with every movement and sound. If you do this the cure will certainly take place; the cure as the healing of illnesses or wounds, and also the cure as the caring and nurturing of the whole being, where we experience a full spiritual charge, a flourishing or a self-sufficient vitality. This deep cure can come into being only when full enlightenment is attained and actualized with total freedom. For such enlightenment eradicates all forms of distortion regarding perceptions, thoughts and opinions, as well as utterly destroying the compulsive-obsessive character structures.

The last point that I would like to make clear is the relationship between release and cure. With release we are applying the remedy and undertaking treatment. The experience is both pleasant and unpleasant. At the same time we are nourished with flashes of insight, like lightning, into our personal histories and the fundamental issues affecting our lives. When the cure takes place, the release has completed its process and the thunder of wisdom comes into full actualization with all its enormous strength and power. This is the end of Dukkha, pain and suffering, which means a healthy existence. Then a new life begins to emanate and takes full charge of our organism.

2.

MEDITATION AND EXPLOSION

To explode is to burst out spontaneously, to release suddenly and to cut powerfully through all the things that obstruct and block the natural, free flow of energies within our body and mind. In explosion there is an element of destruction, not in the sense of action associated with certain negative states, such as anger, hatred, envy, jealousy and hostility, but the utter, cleansing destruction which leaves no ashes behind, but only clears away accumulated debris.

Motive and self-determination will not be found in the act of exploding. In other words, it is a true miracle, occurring unexpectedly and surprisingly. This kind of destruction has no destroyer. So long as a destroyer exists, there is motive, plan, purpose and reason for his action. A destroyer's actions can never be spontaneous or pure. Everything the destroyer does becomes a bondage, a thing which he has to pay for in some way. He is completely bound and tied up with his actions. This is what we call 'karma'. So the destroyer cannot escape suffering, no matter how hard he tries to do so. His position is like an elephant stuck in the mud. The more the elephant attempts to get out of the mud, the deeper he sinks into it.

The other aspect of explosion lies in the positive and joyful experiences of meditation – joy, bliss, ecstasy, sudden stillness of the mind, motionlessness and lightness of the body, the ending of thought, a deep and profound silence within, etc. If you watch closely and attentively to what is actually happening during meditation, you will see this exploding process operating with sensitive, vital awareness. For instance, when watching the movement of your breath with complete, unbroken attention for some time, you suddenly perceive nothing apart from a pure movement in which creation is taking place with enormous strength and powerful energy. This usually happens at the point of the highest intensity of passive watchfulness, when the meditator or watcher disappears completely.

Sometimes, we see the sudden disappearing of thought, a dropping away of the thinking mind and reactive feeling. Then we find ourselves in a totally new, vast and deep place where there is no recognition whatsoever. Time and space vanish altogether, and there is no dimension to be perceived; there is no centre for being. It is a delightful stretch of level ground. After coming out of such meditation, you are always astonished with the passing of time and the profound sense of awakening. The body is motionless and light with no aches or pains, but completely normal in its functioning. At other times, you find the body full of sweat but with a pleasant sensation. In both cases, you feel clean, clear and pure. This is the beauty of explosion in meditation.

At psychological and emotional levels, we see an explosion taking place in sudden and spontaneous expression in meditation as a natural means of cleansing the karmic accumulations at these levels of existence. In the body, for instance, we find many different holding points or blockages obstructing the flow of energy, vitality and life, so that many of us cannot actually function properly as human beings; sometimes we cannot even manage to break down. In order to be liberated at all levels – physical, emotional, psychological, social, mental and spiritual – we have to deal with every aspect of our lives, our pain and suffering. If any part is neglected, total freedom will remain a dream.

How does expression as explosion in meditation work?

Those who are not familiar with my work often think that there are techniques used to induce certain states. This is not true. In fact, all students of mine are instructed to begin in the traditional, cross-legged position, paying attention to all that arises, watching the movement of the breath and the expansion and contraction of the body. During the periods of sitting, mindfully walking and keeping silent, the meditative energy, technically known as 'ātāpa', is naturally developed. It moves through the whole body, penetrating and pushing through the areas where negative, destructive energies are held locked. In this way, the process of cleansing begins to take place by itself. Aches and pain in certain parts of the body may indicate that there is something wrong there, not only physically, but also psychologically and emotionally. Only clear, sensitive awareness can tell us what is happening, and this will come about if we can stay with the pain, not seeking to avoid it but giving permission for whatever there is to expose itself. Sometimes this entails a sudden release of energy, either in sound or with movement.

But there is no self-determination and planning of what we do or how to achieve effects. We just let things be and see what happens, facing whatever arises with total attention and without discrimination. In Buddhist terminology we can say that it is a state of consciousness acting itself out, releasing its negative material and purifying itself. Here we are able to see in action the Buddha's teaching of *anattā* or no-self, precisely because there is no actor behind the action, no expressor behind the expression, no feeler behind the feeling, and so on. The so-called meditator is a witness, a provider of hospitality. Then insight into the story contained and concentrated in such a holding point reveals the truth of the person's karma as deposited conditioning. With the release of such karma, clarity, lightness, and free flow of energy, or freedom for being, are achieved spontaneously and naturally, though not without a great deal of hard work in enduring and exerting energy. In this way we can see that there are two meditative processes going on simultaneously: the elimination or purification, and the cultivation or development, both in body and mind.

Of course, we also encounter many problems when we are totally open to ourselves in this kind of meditation. All the hidden tendencies and repressed feelings, as well as fears and deep grief, may resurface. Furthermore, the psychological freedom that results sometimes brings about the excitement of the ego, and the meditator may then get caught up in this game, involving himself with the process, which can lead to performance and self-indulgence. But with constant awareness and guidance, one leaves the detour and returns to the free way of *Vipassana*.

Another problem lies in becoming attached to negativity, to one's suffering. Again, with attention, awareness and appropriate instruction, you will gain insight into what is happening and then move out of the dark place and take further steps towards liberation.

In working with energy in meditation, it is essential for us to be totally open and be willing to surrender, because the act of surrendering will help us to go beyond our ego level of existence. At least it does not give support to the ego to act. In this way surrendering becomes a powerful means of opening the channels. We can use another metaphor by saying that we provide hospitality for the energy to work. So providing hospitality is the same as surrendering. It is giving up your struggle for achievement and accomplishment, so there is no goal in mind. There is only opening to experience, which could come or could happen anytime. In other words, we allow the pure action or the genuine experience to come to us.

But whatever happens in the negative or the positive way happens because it is bound to happen or because it comes into the moment. If you can really surrender and provide this total hospitality by just staying with awareness and watchfulness and allowing anything to happen without interfering or getting involved with what is happening, then the energy can work through more powerfully and more effectively. If there are any negative energy states to clear up, then they will clear up. If there is just a flow of awareness without having any obstructions in the flow of the body and mind, then there will be positive experience of stillness and deep silence. It is a way of transcending superficial states of consciousness. And all of this comes because of the energy, and not because of trying to make it happen. Trying to make it happen does not produce the true experience. Sometimes it becomes a sort of self-creation of the mind in order to satisfy itself. But we can be deceived by mental creations. It is hard to judge what is the genuine experience and what is not. But you can see by the way you come to experience or the way experience comes to you. If you are totally nothing, you are not creating, you are not acting, and you become totally one with awareness.

Then surely any experience, whether positive or negative, will be real and genuine. It may surprise you as you do not expect these things to happen. So it is very important that you are able to surrender to energy. Energy is being generated when one is silent, sitting or walking, or undertaking any movement in the meditative state. Energy works sometimes through obstacles, but often we cannot perceive this. Also, we get involved in the things that hinder the cleaning-up process, or indeed with the process itself; the result is that we do not look beyond the bursting or the final emergence from the negative states.

But if you learn to stay with awareness more and more, then it gets sharper and clearer and you see experience, and even beyond experience to something different. In that sense there is no concept of the experiencer involved with whatever experience that takes place. It is a matter of allowing oneself to become one with awareness – to be awareness, but not to be a person who is aware. By transcending this concept of person, you allow more and more inner strength, clarity, and power. You may call it personal power because it is your ability to express and to get into experience fully. It is the ability to peel off inhibitions and self-consciousness, allowing the totality of being to emerge or actualize itself without having the second person to interfere. It is important to be totally with awareness, every moment with non-action, doing nothing. When being quiet or going anywhere, if you keep that awareness through the movement of your life, it becomes a powerful tool for dealing with any of your problems or with any form of negative energy. It allows you to get into deep experience very quickly and naturally.

We talk about surrendering. Another word connected with that is submission. You have to understand the difference between these two terms. We use 'surrender' in the spiritual experience, but in everyday living, in relationship, we use the term 'submission'. Surrendering does not require authority. There is no authority to which you surrender. Energy, what we call powerful energy, is not authority; you surrender to that energy not because you are afraid, or because you want something from that energy, or because you want to satisfy something. You simply allow yourself to be there. Surrender is like throwing yourself into fire. You can throw yourself into fire without expecting anything. The act of throwing oneself into something powerful is the act of allowing oneself to experience oneself totally with the help of powerful energy. When powerful energy is available, we can surrender and let go of our struggling, our desire to act, our desire to work something out. So in that way you do not have authority in your mind. You do not expect either reward or punishment, but just give yourself totally to the moment when something is happening.

If there is any resistance then it can be seen. Resistance is usually less when there is willingness to give and be vulnerable. Before coming to that point of willingness there might be some resistance, which we can watch without resisting by just allowing them to come. If you resist your resistances then you have double work. We have to allow things to flow. Everything is allowed because it is a phenomenon – the sun, wind, rain, clouds, whatever. You cannot stop the wind from blowing. It stops by itself, when there is no condition for blowing. When we do not understand that process we try to get hold of everything. We try to control all phenomena and all things within us, which we cannot do. Then we feel we do not have power. We do not have power to deal with our conditioning, our habits, and our tendencies; those things become habits because they succeed in making us feel that we do not have power, and so they gain the power to dominate. So then, how do personal power and inner strength come to us?

The first thing is to allow ourselves to be whatever we are, and be open to experience, willing to embrace anything that comes to us. With no choice, we can equally embrace the ugly and the beautiful. If you have that ability, then you have the strength and the power to meet challenges and to express yourself. The ability to express oneself is to allow oneself to get into experience and to make that experience known to oneself clearly.

Just allowing, without intending to do so, creates the channels for the flow of personal power. It gives inner strength to act and to cope with whatever is happening. Then there is no lack of power. In that sense we are totally ourselves, but there is no strong, solid identity to cling to. There is simply a feeling of being oneself which satisfies the needs of identity.

The need for identity is very strong in human beings, but true identity – the totality of being – happens by itself so we do not need to worry about losing identity. You allow more inner strength to flow; inner strength is always connected with all spiritual factors, which means all the natural spontaneous things in life. This means not going along with the conditioned state, because being a conditioned person you are identified with a certain culture. When you are a product of certain conditions of family, society, then you have to act according to their demands so that you cannot be yourself. When you conform to the requirements of others there is no personal power or inner strength to act genuinely, purely and spontaneously. We lose spontaneity and choice, because of conforming – because of being a conditioned person.

Working against conditioning is hard. In a way, we do not work against conditioning; rather, we recognize the conditions in us and how they work within us. Such non-performing and bare attention opens the door to inner strength, power, clarity, our awareness – anything which is not the conditioned state. So we become aware of our conditioned state of being and allow our unconditioned state to come, not trying to break conditions by force or will, but just letting them be and watching them the whole time. When all the creative, healthy things are allowed to grow and come into operation more and more, then the conditioned states will die away gradually. So we have to keep watching our old states and allowing our new states to develop and actualize themselves, to come to light and to act in our life more and more.

But sometimes we get caught up in our conditioned state, attached to our negativity, and do not allow our new states to operate in our lives or to move on with the beautiful and creative things we encounter. Mainly, this is due to a lack of trust. We do not trust anything that is new, growing or emerging. When this happens the strength of the conditioned states is much stronger. Then we give in by way of giving power to the conditioned states and by not flowing with the new thing we have. The conditioning is pulling and pushing us in a way. But if we learn to flow with the new understanding, the new freedom, the new insights into life – the something new that is growing and blossoming within us – then surely these things will become bigger, larger, more powerful, while the negative, destructive, and unhealthy things wither and die. These two processes work together – the process of eliminating, which means letting the conditioned states die away and the process of cultivating, growing, and allowing the natural and spontaneous things to flow unhindered.

In a way we are not growing or cultivating anything; we are allowing these things to come. When we allow within ourselves, the channels of growth and development are opened. Allowing is a very powerful word, and a very powerful action. The message should be: 'Now allow yourself to be who you are'. Allow yourself to sit, allow yourself to watch, to walk, to be aware – to give permission to yourself to do this. Then you will see that you are flowing with awareness.

Awareness can put us in touch with things, help us to grow and to move on. Awareness can be induced with any exercise, any technique or during any action; it can be done whilst breathing, chanting, dancing, cooking, cleaning, washing dishes, or anything, so that we have all the opportunities for cultivating awareness that we need. Even when we are lying down, we can be aware of what is happening. The flow of action, of getting in touch with whatever arises is a very simple one. Everything is so accessible. Nothing is far away. Even the whole universe is accessible. In this way, we attain harmony with our environment and with the universe. When we feel things are far away, it is because we are in the mind, enmeshed in the concept, and not in awareness.

It is, then, a matter of allowing – allowing anything to happen, allowing ourselves to be, allowing others to be, so that there is no judgement and no sense of being obstructed or barred by what is happening in the environment. We strengthen our awareness all the time, whether things are happening within us or without us. Then we find more capacity, more personal power to remain ourselves totally in all situations, and to make contact with our quietness and stillness, even among noises. When you allow things to happen, they stay on the surface, but *you* are deep down within your being. All too often we invent a dwelling-place and stay there so that we cannot sink down to the depths. With the attitude of allowing, you can flow with energy – the energy of awareness. Such energy has intelligence, clarity, alertness and intuitive wisdom. Just let it lead and act.

Although explosion is a very natural thing in meditation, we must not over-emphasize it by taking it as a prerequisite in our approach. This could lead to anticipation and expectation of the expressive explosion taking place at each meditational sitting. Any form of expectation is self-performance and self-indulgence. Any attempt to produce something in meditation is not the right action; it becomes an obstacle to the natural unfolding of reality. What we can produce and create is unreality, for the real can only reveal itself when all our efforts come to an end and when all the conditioned states stand still without interfering with the movement of the unknowable, from which our true wisdom springs.

When we allow ourselves to be totally vulnerable to everything that we encounter – to our fears, our joys, pleasures, peace, lovingness, kindness, gentleness, happiness, compassion, and humility – then they can expose themselves to us naturally. We become channels through which things can flow unobstructed and without any resistances, rather than containers. For vulnerability to be, there must be unconditional openness and freedom from self-conceptualization and self-consciousness. In other words, one must become absolutely nothing; that is to say, being oneself *completely*, without a second person (our solid reality) sitting somewhere within the body and mind to direct the course of our behaviour. With such vulnerability, explosion comes, the whole truth reveals itself and inward light shines forth, so that there is no place to hide and nothing can possibly be hidden. Only open and empty space prevails and permeates the entire being.

Sometimes in meditation you have many things to watch: thoughts, feelings, mental pictures, fantasies. If you carry on watching them with no sense of choice, and without trying to stop or overcome them, all of a sudden, everything drops away and the mind becomes totally still and yet completely awake. This is a natural explosion in meditation. It hits you like a sudden storm. The movement of creation begins to spread out with vast, unlimited and immense creative energy. Here is the gathering, the coming together of all essential inner resources pertaining to enlightenment. The total revelation of Truth, with all its attributes, comes into being simultaneously with the utter destruction of compulsive desire, obsessive becoming and passionate ignorance – the ignorance that darkens consciousness and blinds the mind, preventing it from seeing clearly what is really happening at any given moment.

3.

BUDDHA AND THE PRINCIPLE OF CONTACT

Life is a series of contacts – physical, emotional and spiritual. Contact is ever-present and implies movement. Everything is moving: the Universe; the Earth, the Sun, the stars, and each of us. This constant state of movement is the basis of contact. Everything is relative. Energy, too, is movement. Without movement there can be no perception. We move, vibrate, to provide a basis for contact with reality, to be in the world of relationships. This contact provides a common ground for communication, for rendering experience intelligible, and for feeling the flow of life.

Contact creates feelings and sensations. The eyes come into contact with a visible object and sensation arises, with attendant feelings. This relationship applies to all the senses, including what might be called the mind sense. When we meditate, we enter the world of the mind. This includes the emotions, feelings, perceptions and everything that conditions our lives and consciousness, including the states that arise in consciousness itself. We move into contact with both the mental and physical worlds; for example, experiencing the discomforts of our bodies during long sitting. When we contact experiences from the past, conditioned patterns of perception, and emotion, we react. But if we avoid contact with our minds and bodies, there is no life, but a feeling of deadness. Contact brings either pleasure or pain. This is experience.

What happens when these feelings arise? When there is feeling, there is desire – desire either to obtain the object or to be rid of it. Desire can go in two directions, depending on the feeling. If feeling is pleasurable, we want to hold on, leading to the process of becoming: we may have a flash of something like enlightenment and immediately desire to hold onto the good feeling and *become* it. Negative states and bad feelings, lead to the desire of not-having, destroying, removing, or avoiding, and put us into conflict. We are in conflict with the desire to enjoy. This struggle can bring the taste of truth. We see that feeling is a condition for desire, and that desire leads to a struggle to achieve, to bring about and satisfy. This process can lead us in any of three directions: into constructive action, destructive action, or non-action.

What supports desire? What keeps it going and gives it the power to dominate? Clinging and attachment. The more we desire, the more we become attached. Even in the desire to run away, there is attachment – attachment to running. In detachment, there is desire and attachment as well. For detachment, in the sense of becoming indifferent and avoiding, becomes a neurotic reaction to negative attachment. It represents an attitude of non-confrontation in the face of that which is undesirable. There are many forms of attachment; but they all lead to karma.

There is attachment to views, ideas, opinions; and attachment to ritual, ceremony, activities that lead to pleasant, high states of mind, or purity of body. It may be, with certain rituals, that you can even experience enlightenment, or achieve union with the One. That, too, is attachment. There is attachment to the ego, the self. This results in not wanting to see things objectively, as they are, but as certain images, fixed identities – including ourselves, as a fixed identity. It comes from seeking the reassurance of feeling one's existence. That kind of attachment is very subtle and difficult to break. Very difficult, because we feel we survive through our identity,

through an identification with something. Ego is identification
– the act of identifying with things, ideas, names, form,
position, status.

Attachment deepens desire. Desire is a fire and attachment
is the fuel that feeds the fire. Because of attachment, there is
the karma process – the process of doing and becoming, and
we have an accumulation of karma. There are two forms of
what we call *bhava* in Pali: the process of karma *bhava*, the wilful
intention to act, to become involved through doing, which
includes mental activities. This is the first form. This karma
process leads to different accumulations: habits, feelings,
emotions, anger, hatred, resentment and the suppression of
these feelings. It leads also to knowledge, faith and intention-
ality. These qualities are created through attachment, and lead
to the state of becoming, the second category in the *bhava*
process. The process of karma and the process of becoming go
together. You do and feel this; you become that. It is a
continuous cycle that increases our conditioning. That is how
desire and attachment support the karma process. And this
process supports our actions in the world.

Everyone accumulates karma. There is the karma of ignorance, of not seeing reality and lacking understanding. Because
of this ignorance, we lack insight into our processes and
repress our feelings, accumulating anger, self-hatred and
resentment, with great suffering as a result. But clear seeing
eliminates habitual patterns and repression. Without this clear
seeing, we tend to become fixed, compulsive and boxed in.
Ignorance operates to prevent us from seeing this cycle. Then
suffering becomes necessary to bring us around to paying
attention. This ignorance is the seat of conditioning. As we
condition ourselves, *sankara* arises – the accumulated pro-
grammes in the self. These two processes – ignorance and
sankara – support the attachment-desire cycle, and the whole
karma process, or process of becoming. This karma process
works with conditioning and ignorance, desire and attachment;
these then become the five causes of conditioned existence.
With the causes, come the five effects: consciousness,
body/mind, the six senses, contact and feeling.

I use the term consciousness to refer to rebirth consciousness. At the moment of conception, consciousness arises, followed by name and form, which develop into the mind and body of an individual. With the mind and body come the senses – five physical and one mental – for communication with the world. Everything is provided for the communicating process to arise. That is what is most wonderful about being human. However, it creates a great challenge as well, for inevitable complications will arise in the process of attempting to make contact. We become a particular person, a Mr X or a Ms Y. The birth of 'I am' is the birth of ego, recognizing its own existence as a conventional truth. As your hair and your organs and your whole body proceed with growth after birth, so does the ego proceed with the attachment to being a person, a particular individual. This growth is a decay, at the same time. Where there is life, there is death. It is unavoidable at every point. So old age and death come into being at the very moment of birth. Because of being born, it is said, lamentation and grief come into existence. In Pali, birth brings the arising of *soka*, sorrow; *parideva*, lamentation; *dukkha*, pain; *domanasa*, grief; and *upayasa*, despair. These comprise *dukkha* – the suffering that attends being born, beginning with contact, as the basis of experience. We must look at life that way.

It is very important to see how *dukkha* arises. In a life of contact and feeling, with desire and attachment attending us at every moment, we must have awareness. Awareness helps us to avoid the tricks of ignorance, by attending to what is happening, seeing and understanding it. With the awareness of the karma process and the process of doing and becoming, we will attain full understanding. Even without full understanding, we will still have insight into our conditioning and our state of being and how to proceed for wisdom to flow with awareness. Awareness includes the perception of our limitations, our ignorance. We must not avoid our dark side. When we meditate, we look at our behaviour patterns, our reactions, our habits – in short, our conditioning. We see how we are blocked, mentally and physically, how we become inhibited, and how we are not free to respond and to be, naturally. We can see how karma has been accumulated in certain parts of our minds and bodies. This perception is a clarifying practice.

Everyone is born into a life of duality, with dualistic qualities within themselves. These qualities cannot be destroyed, although they can be transcended. In the conventional sense, good and evil, black and white, all dualities, are concepts. But in reality, there is only energy. If energy has a negative quality, awareness will eventually allow positive energy to flow. To this extent the body and mind are always pure. So, rather than destroying negative energy, we allow it to flow through and change to creative energy. By allowing this natural process to occur, we cleanse our burdens away. This is the process that occurs with the meditative state of mind.

By transcending good and evil, I mean to avoid the concepts of good and evil. These concepts are connected with conventional rules. You can be liberated from conventional rules by seeing reality – not by following an *idea* of liberation, but by looking deeply into what good is, what evil is, free of mental concepts. When we describe the enlightened state of mind as good, we are giving an interpretation. It is good because we like it and aspire to it. When we say is is a good state of mind, we mean that we want to escape negativity. But even negative, destructive states are good, in the sense that they help us to become awakened to their effect, their reality, and so to a way out of them. Without these unhappy states, we would remain unmotivated. Letting go of concepts of good and evil can be called social liberation – being liberated from social rules, conventions. This is connected to inner liberation, being free from ignorance and conditioning, and the whole karmic process we have accumulated in our lives. Within us, then, there are no disturbing influences. Things become peaceful and clear. Then it is easier for us to become liberated from those social standards that limit our inner peace and expansiveness, the rules that confine us to a narrow space in life.

Now we can see the reverse order of the twelve links, progressing from *dukkha* to death. When there is no ignorance, there is no conditioning. When there is no conditioning, there is no consciousness, in the sense of rebirth consciousness. When there is no rebirth consciousness, there is no mind and body, as a conditioning process. When there is no mind and body, there are no six sense organs. When there are no six sense organs, there is no contact. When there is no contact, there is no feeling. With no feeling, there is no desire. No desire, no attachment. No attachment, no karma process and no process of becoming. Then, there is no birth. When there is no birth, there is no death. That is *the process of the cessation of dukkha*.

Ignorance is the key; for when it goes, karma and conditioning cannot operate. The five causes are transcended, although we can still use the positive energy of ignorance, conditioning, attachment, desire and becoming for functioning in the world. But *they* can no longer use *us*. That is the meaning of being liberated.

The end of *dukkha* is found in the arising of *dukkha*. If you see the arising, you can see the end; otherwise, it is not possible to see the ending of it. That is why our work is to pay attention to how things arise; how pain arises; how suffering arises; how anger arises. Seeing puts an end to the process. If there is ignorance and unclear seeing, then we have to look again, more deeply. Go into it and stay there, watching, penetrating deeply into what is happening, and you will understand the whole structure of the process.

To see *dukkha* is not pleasant. That is why expression comes. Seeing fear, rage, and control by others creates bad feeling. This negative feeling may have such force that it must be expressed. But we must also see that we are not carried away by expression: it must become another object for awareness. We attend to what is happening in the process of expressing. With full seeing, how can we fall into suffering? Seeing clearly means seeing reality, not seeing with theory or knowledge of one kind or another. Seeing in perfect wisdom at the point of arising leads to liberation. That is wisdom. Wisdom is strength. Wisdom is the cutting edge that pierces, penetrates and cuts off. That is the way of vipassana: developing wisdom, being constantly aware, and seeing again and again, until there is nothing more to be seen. Then see whether there is liberation.

There are two kinds of *dukkha* processes, an old process and a present process. The old process is contained in our minds and bodies, accumulated as karma. (But karma is a part of *dukkha*. *Dukkha* covers both pain and pleasure, joy and sorrow.)

Present *dukkha* is connected with conditioning: social conditioning refers to all the accumulated traditions and education. Personal conditioning comes from our own karma, the rebirth consciousness. Personal conditioning is contained in the mind; but social conditioning is contained in the mind and body. For example, in our bodies we can see and feel the results of having to conform to social rules, such as the rule of not expressing negative responses. If we control against expressing bad feelings, we can feel our muscles contract and tense up. These body knots form our conditioned patterns arising from social rules and our tendency to conform to social rules. We create this conditioning out of the need for feeling pleasure. That is the way pleasure becomes part of the *dukkha* process, leading to karmic process. Another example is conforming to a social habit of comfort which leads to sitting and reclining on soft surfaces, resulting in loss of structural integration of the body.

This is the karma we create for ourselves, in our own bodies. We find pains, tensions, knotted muscle tissue, and the need to heal our bodies. Exercise and body work then become part of the meditative process. If we avoid this aspect of the work, being tired or lazy, we stop caring for ourselves and our well-being. But following through with body work gives lightness and clarity and relaxation of the body. It keeps you in touch with the body processes and with the different levels that tension can reach. Our work is to bring this tension to the surface, to awareness. This is vipassana yoga. Sitting brings us in touch wth the mind and the emotions at a personal and social level. Vipassana yoga connects us with the muscles and physical system of karma, so that we can cleanse out every knot and clear out our body karma. If we have twenty, thirty, or forty years to go, we can start now working constantly to cleanse the body. But we must remain aware of the fact that no particular technique or idea is a complete practice for body clearing, nor an end in itself. Rolfing, or the Alexander technique, or patterning and sensory awareness do not lead in themselves to a cleared-out body. For when we stop a technique for a certain time, the body does not stay clear. That means there must be constant attention to our bodies, and to the maintenance of good balance and clarity in our physical system.

The same is true of the mind. The mind can cause trouble, because it is full of ideas, rules and fixations, philosophies and knowledge. Then we cannot be open to the reality of the moment. We carry ideas and knowledge as a burden, placed in the head. We must do this, or be that way, because some Buddhist doctrine says so, or some Taoist text, or some other form of knowledge dictates it. Knowledge can be useful in achieving concrete things, like building a house, or driving a car. But real suffering arises when we know a theory, but do not know how to put it into practice, or refuse to put it into practice. Conflict results and we must accept the consequences of our ignorance.

Life requires constant attention, whether we are standing, sitting, moving, lying down, or doing anything. If we know what is really happening, and catch the tendency to respond to it, we bring about cessation. For example, if we do something wrong, and feel bad about having done so, we can watch how it came about. With attention and learning we cease to be victimized by our very own actions. We must accept the possibility of making mistakes, but we can learn from the ones we make, which will eventually lead to right action. This is the practice of looking at the *dukkha* process, in meditation and in life.

Whatever it is that we do, whether we are a professor or a housewife or a carpenter, we will learn from the situation life presents to us. We can also watch what happens in inter-personal relationships. How do others affect us? Peoples' opinions, ideas, criticisms. *Dukkha* is everywhere and in every contact. *Dukkha* is the small black dot in the middle of pleasure. If we do not watch it, we will be carried away and suffer when things change. With awareness, there is no clinging when things pass. With awareness, you can enjoy things, and be free of them when they pass. We can practise giving freedom to the object of our pleasure, letting it move away from us, without feeling frustration. That is a kind of generosity, which includes being generous with ourselves, without feeling guilty, as well as feeling generous to others.

We can see what gives us pleasure, and what makes us suffer. This could be anything in the world. There is so much. Why cling to one object? Without clinging, we cannot become victims of any object, or its passing away. Something may be lost, but there are no broken hearts. The heart breaks because of not understanding, not letting go. We are left with an emotional wound. The heart regains its health when it is generous and free. Then love will flow. The more love there is, the more love we give out, the more generous we become. We are no longer miserly, but become expansive in the world, feeling that our space just spreads out farther and farther. We can become the whole universe.

Frustration arises from wanting and not having something. If we give ourselves many possibilities we can flow on. If we feel bound to only one thing or one person, we cannot flow; we become obstructed and frustrated. But we can experience loss without frustration if we allow ourselves to flow on to other things. Loss can be experienced positively, showing us our strengths and weaknesses, as well as new possibilities.

The end of *dukkha* is found in the experience of *dukkha*. Without the experience, how can *dukkha* come to an end? Some people say that you meditate to pay off your karmic debt. But just sitting, looking for an end to karma, is a vague process. It is not a matter of paying off the debt; but of withdrawing the deposit! When you do not keep a deposit, you can destroy the bank. Then everything becomes clear.

Vipassana is a journey of discovery. It is a full-time job, not just for weekend retreats, or for the duration of a single meditative sitting; but for every moment, and with every breath. If you do it, surely you will be free. Awakening comes to you because you are totally aware of everything. Without alertness, you become sleepy and clouded. The hardest thing about Vipassana is that it has no rules. We must rely on understanding to guide us. Life is very real; and it is good to approach it with a realistic attitude, rather than with optimism or pessimism. When we arrive at the point of seeing what is actually taking place, everything is accessible. You feel intimate with everything. That attitude brings a feeling of oneness. You just reach out and everything is touchable.

Life takes on new meaning when we come to apportion blame. We should not blame desires, attachment, karma, or ignorance and conditioning. We should simply acknowledge them and look at what they do to us, seeing how free we can be in relation to them. This is the point. If we look constantly, we can catch them even when they seem to be hiding within. The goal of life becomes the living of it.

After a retreat, or in everyday life, you can review yourself to check how much work you have done to make a foundation you can work from – not just to measure how much has been achieved, cleared up and eliminated; but how much remains to be cleared up. This is very important. Sometimes measuring how close to enlightenment one is, or indeed how far away, is wrong thinking in that it causes either suffering or pride. We should be realistic about the work we have to do on ourselves and keep the awareness focused on that. Enlightenment is just an ideal. Thinking about it simply promotes fantasy. We have to be scrupulously honest with ourselves. We should not regard the process as being finished or unfinished; we should simply wait and see.

If we have negative feelings, we should look closer at them. They are always connected with some idea or expectation in our mind. On recognizing the cause, we can let it go. If we return negative feeling with negative feeling, it is a reaction that causes more karma. A negative reaction to a negative state feeds the state itself, deepening it. You have to realize that you are not the doer. If you identify with the doer, then you cease to look at him. There is just reaction. The doer is the pattern, the conditioning, even though this operates within your mind and body, which you might call yourself. You can have total communication with what arises in your mind and body, or you can see if there is lack of it and misunderstanding. Communication does not mean that you have conversations with the doer; but that you move together towards understanding. The doer and you can realize the truth together.

You can trust the body to give you good advice. There is intelligent energy in the body, if we stay in touch with it. Sometimes, if you stay with the body, you can transcend it and experience a feeling of being uplifted into pure energy. Then heaviness and tensions drop. As long as we are in the world we accumulate tension; but we also have the means to keep clearing it up.

4.

DISCIPLINE AND LEARNING

Discipline is essential for challenging the ego. Generally speaking, the ego does not like discipline. But some egos pretend to have discipline in order to avoid contact or to feel more comfortable, creating a narrow, small world in which to live and shutting off all the possibility of interaction with other egos. Negative feelings, fears and repressions can thus be kept turned inward. Such egos also cling to rigid inflexibility living by the rules without really paying attention to the actual situations of life both within and outside. They become goal-oriented and keep themselves away from digging deeply into their anthills of body and mind.

The attempt to observe discipline can cause tensions and distractions inside oneself. Then a person finds it hard to relax, and without relaxation there is no clarity of insight into the real nature of things. At a retreat, we create discipline to challenge the ego, putting it into that situation to see what it can do and how it reacts. You then watch the reactions of the ego with all its compulsions and impulses coming out with the reactive processes.

Is it possible for the ego to react if certain conditions do not feed it from behind? How can you be free from your reactions? Is there any possibility for just responding and acting with spontaneity, total perception, simplicity and clarity? Certainly, when things become simple. Action is then performed with the flow of insight or understanding at the moment. This means that the immediate perception of something brings about an action. Such a perception is not a condition for the action. In actual fact, the immediate and total perception itself is creative action. What we normally call action afterwards is the continuation of that perception. It goes into operation, actualizing what it perceives. In this way, we have no one to drive us, to tell us what to do and what not to do. So long as we are bound by conditions, we always have somebody behind us, looking over our shoulders – internalized authority or inner voices – directing our course of action.

By making conversations, we tend to live in the past and avoid the present; this dispenses energy that is necessary for the meditative work. In order to conserve energy for meditating, we need to observe silence creatively. In the atmosphere of creative silence, you can see many things stirred up or manifested, such as projections onto people's reactions, anxieties about making noises, feeling self-conscious, compulsive patterns of escaping oneself and seeking out others for one's own pleasure and security. On the positive side, we find silence as the means for renewing our consciousness and deepening our intuitive wisdom, as well as for sinking down into deeper peace and tranquillity. Random conversation is a form of sleep, which is pleasant to the ego, particularly to the talkative ego who cannot survive without keeping its mouth busy. Clinging to psychological sleep will deepen our ignorance and obstruct our natural flow towards awakening.

We sleep psychologically without knowing what we are doing. We sleep with knowledge. We sleep with method and technique. We sleep with traditions and culture. We sleep with dreams and fantasies. We sleep with ideals, ideas and ideologies. We sleep with conversations and inner talking. We do not look and listen and see clearly what is happening. Our senses are blurred, unclear, non-radiant and therefore not receptive. That is why we need awareness and alertness so as to enable us to cleanse all those impurities and conditioned states called deposited karma which block the natural flow of intelligence and wisdom, as well as the flow of life. We need to provide hospitality for creative energy to work with awareness and insight by sitting, walking, keeping silent, being physically alone without any companions, being in touch with whatever is occurring both internally and externally in every moment. That is your hospitality provided for the work of *ātāpa* energy, which has the quality of burning, cleaning out and putting away all the barriers, obstructions and blockages, including dust and dirt in our psycho-physical system. That energy will generate mainly in the sittings, walkings, body work and through silence. We can see that if we get into complete inward silence, we shall find tremendous energy and vitality generated and flowing out within our organism.

With the movement of such energy, the negative, destructive and unhealthy states of mind, including repressive emotions and all the stories connected with them, will be stirred up and relived so that the purification can take place. Then, creative energy and healthy and constructive states of consciousness will flow in and grow with beauty, love and luminosity. Through these processes the direct knowing of facts and realities arises spontaneously. There is no question of 'How can I know?' That question is an excuse for not allowing all explorations and explosions to do their work, and for not going into complete silence both inwardly and outwardly. We are afraid that if we do not talk we will not exist and will be unable to identify ourselves. While talking, whether inner or outer, you feel you are somebody; you are conscious of identity. But when you keep silent mindfully, you come close to yourself and get scared. You think: 'What is going to happen? Something powerful is coming toward me. I am going to lose my mind.' You cling to your mind, believing what it says, so that you cannot let it go. Certainly, the mind will fight inch by inch for its own survival. Those who stay outside of the actual experience, and who conform compulsively to whatever conditions the mind creates, may say that you are crazy. It does not matter what people say so long as you know what is happening. You do not have to be influenced by people's ideas and attitudes or their ways of behaving and reacting.

It is essential for us to sink down into that well of silence and see how it feels. Sometimes you feel that the inner dialogue does not stop and seems to go on and on. But at other times it does stop briefly. If you try to make it stop, you may succeed. But you then create your personal pride which will become a fetter binding you to greed and attachment. If you just let it drop, by simply staying with full awareness and flowing with your breath, you don't get too excited, but maintain balance and equilibrium so that no pride or self-importance will be invented. Then there is a free flow of the natural unfolding.

With regard to the breathing, it is interesting to note that each time we breathe we take in not only the air, but the energy of our environment. Energy is being taken in with each breath: therefore there will be no lack of pure energy when staying at a place surrounded by trees, hills, lakes and very clean air. When we breathe in such things, the creative energy goes inside and helps us to get in touch with our inner resources, penetrating the obstacles and blockages in both body and mind. Then the cleansing or purifying process will begin to work. With awareness and creative energy operating inside, the negative and destructive things will be pushed out through the out-breathing and the spontaneous expressions.

When we go into deep meditation, with complete inward silence, we need little air, for unnecessary air can become a distressing factor in such a meditative state. It is natural for a meditator to need less and less air and to breathe evenly and silently when in a deep state of meditation. There is no personal intention involved with that occurrence. It is the matter of the organism planning its way through its own wisdom. So if you continue to flow with the even motion of your breath and keep your awareness clear and alert, you can feel energy coming through the breathing and experience something flowing out and being released. Sometimes, you notice minor irritations in certain parts of the body, or perhaps some pain coming out with the breathing. But larger karmic deposits may burst out in a different way. Nevertheless, it is through breathing that we get in touch with things within us. Then the *ātāpa* energy is being generated, admitting the new pure energy into the work. That is why you do not have to act or to do anything or to try to make things happen. You just provide hospitality and become totally passive at the ego level and then the complete surrendering to the *ātāpa* energy and wisdom will come into force. The ego may not be passive, but it can be watched.

Ego is the compulsive pattern of conditioning arising at the point of identification. If you keep watching your conditioning and go through it with full awareness, allowing anything to happen, you will have clear insight into the ego and its functions. Through this way, there is no resisting or fighting: you can find your own space and are able to relate to your ego with clarity.

The Vipassana practice is mind-watching and not mind-control. So, when you watch your mind and see it as it moves and acts, you gain more wisdom and build up your inner strength and the creative power to over-ride the mind. Sometimes you might feel weak and powerless; if you believe this to be true, you give power to the mind. You feed your mind and make it powerful by adhering to what it says. The mind is just the mind. See what the mind is doing and how it creates things. Do not think that the mind is either powerful or powerless, but look instead for a source of pure, creative energy.

Things come up and out because of *ātāpa* energy penetrating, burning, and pushing them out. So when this kind of energy meets an obstacle, it will get burned and have to come out. Particularly in the body, you may feel energy blocks, sometimes accompanied by pain or tension, or you may not be aware of them at all. But when the energy is trying to work out the blockages to clear up tension and pain, the area involved is often hot and even sweating. After that part of the body is clear of the psychological and emotional pain, the body returns to its normal temperature. So we can see that energy is working all the time whether we are aware of it or not. It also burns the mind. The mind becomes restless because it gets burned. The trouble for many people is that when the mind is agitating and roaming about here and there, people become its victim. They impose their preconceptions of how the mind should be on themselves instead of just watching the mind and allowing it to present itself fully so that insights into the mind and mental contents can grow.

Restlessness implies a state of unhappiness, a lack of satisfaction, and is a manifestation of pain. The mind is not satisfied with something. It looks for something pleasurable and enjoyable. When it cannot succeed, it complains and is continually dissatisfied. This is the typical characteristic of a restless mind. But if you look into what is lacking or what the mind is anticipating, you will understand the situation and accept it as it is.

In the Vipassana practice, we have little to do but much to see. Both body and mind become the objects of our meditation. Observe your psycho-physical processes over and over again until they melt away into mere vibrational energy that allows you to transcend them. If this does not happen, keep on watching the body and mind, penetrating into different movements, different activities and various feelings, emotions and thoughts. It is a very simple thing to do. You do not have to look for any technique or method to help you be effective. Sometimes you feel unable to look. Look at the voice that says such a negative thing to you. Then continue looking. You might feel some frustration because of attempting to do what you think you have no ability to do. That is to be looked at too.

Do not avoid frustrations. If you feel frustrated, allow it to happen and remember to look – looking into the causes or conditions that give rise to it. Very often, people try to escape the so-called bad state and try to produce a good one. Clinging to a positive, good state is a very subtle thing in the conditioned mind. But so long as there is a bad state you have to work through it until it melts away. A situation like this is for meeting yourself completely. There is no choice, and no escape. If you react, such a reaction will create more conflict and perpetuate negative patterns of conditioning. It is true that being with yourself all the time for a certain period of time will inevitably lead to boredom, if you find that you are an unpleasant person, or that nothing interesting is happening. Again, in this situation just stay with boredom. You are a bored person, or you are boring yourself. Examine why these conditions prevail. This way of self-understanding, rather than self-conceptualizing, is the way to realize where liberation really lies. Self-concept becomes a stumbling block to total seeing and freedom.

In relating to your environment and to the people around you, it is essential to stay in the state of flowing in and out between yourself and others, to see clearly and precisely how they appear to your perception and how you react to them. You probably want to change the world and people to fit in with your ideas and standards. In certain situations, such as mindfully walking with a group, you might be struggling with your inward comments on someone who is not walking properly or on yourself for your lack of awareness in the present. Watch your reaction and see what is being held in your petty mind.

With the operation of awareness and watchfulness of what is occurring, insightful understanding develops. All the material needed for such growth is here within our human organism. You do not have to look in books to tell you what to do and where to start, or how to go about this matter of growth and maturation. Books are superficial and inadequate in dealing with realities, although they may make it sound very promising. You could also be deceived by the *way* people write. As a result, you try to fit your situation into those described by the so-called experts. The real source of knowledge is your own body and mind, your relationships with yourself, others and the environment. So you cannot avoid the Vipassana way of meditating in your life. It goes with you at every moment and with every activity. Nevertheless, you might lose the Vipassana practice in life when you cease to be attentive and aware.

We can observe, we can look and we can see. The object can be anything or nothing at all. You simply sit and listen to the rain pouring down and you feel cool air on your face. So everything comes into this open field of desireless awareness. You are not blocking, making yourself dead, numb or emotionless. Just let everything come and go. Be totally open and *vulnerable* to everything that is happening, and constantly flow with your awareness. There is no distraction when there is this flow of awareness. Distraction is the outcome of concentration and it comes with desire, such as the desire to be with something or the desire to avoid something or to get something that is not there.

In the practice of Vipassana, the object is not fixed but is allowed to move as freely and as naturally as possible. One does not hold on to the object but learns constantly to apply simple awareness. When you flow with such awareness, the object can come and go like transient phenomena. You then enjoy what is happening from moment to moment, and see the continuity of rising and falling, the endless process of appearing and disappearing. Everything is seen as it is without judging, criticizing, making comments or philosophizing. This is simple awareness.

When breathing, keep your attention on the motion of the breath in your abdomen by feeling the sensation of expansion and contraction. When you breathe in, you feel the air coming into the body and the body expanding or rising. When you breathe out, the air goes out and the belly contracts or falls. Just simply watch these phenomena and get in touch with more energy inside the body. Be totally open to whatever arises whether from within or without. In this way, you do not stay in any fixed, concentrated place but move freely and attentively. Firm but flexible movement and clarity of being become your operating centre, so to speak. As you sit in this kind of centre you can see everything all around without turning sideways or backwards. Allow yourself to be, to feel, to perceive and to experience whatever is available at the moment, whether it is pain, fear, anger, frustration, sadness, joy, bliss, happiness, ecstasy or peace.

Allowance is essentially important. When we do not permit ourselves to look, we cannot see what is actually happening and we automatically try to control or suppress. For instance, when you feel something frightening, you tend to run away or attempt to control yourself, trying to be strong, creating contractions in your muscles and rigid inflexibility in your mind. This is a pattern of avoiding, resisting and obstructing the natural flow of actual experiences. You are then inwardly frozen because fear rules over your personality. When you do not allow yourself to experience the flow and to go through it, fear dominates. Fear is strongest when you are alone. It is when we are alone that we feel susceptible to irrational fears. We think of ghosts and evil spirits when we walk alone in the dark, but the fears are dispersed when other people are with us. Similarly, the things within us come up more strongly when we are isolated and physically alone with ourselves only. Sitting in a group, you are, to some extent, alone in the sense of not communicating with others; nevertheless, you still feel support. When you are absolutely alone somewhere, you may be hit by destructive forces and become powerless, having avoided them for some time. You are not sure what to do and inevitably you become a victim. But if you allow yourself to go through *anything*, and at any time it presents itself, then you can learn to deal with it and bring out your inner strength. Even if you are alone, you can still feel your personal power, reducing the likelihood of victimization. In this way, your own strength and power will become more and more actualized. This is an important point – to see if you are able to exercise your creative power or if you give it away to other people or if you give it to your mind so that you do not have power of your own. Power is essential; it is the creative energy for living our lives and for working with our obstacles or problems of existence.

It is very important to surrender – surrender to the practice of Vipassana, attending to every programme, every group activity: there is no room for excuses or complaints about aches and pains, drowsiness or tiredness. See how far suffering can go. See how much pain can damage the body or how the body can purify itself by going *through* pain and *releasing* pain. There is one thing that tends to create difficulty for us – the tendency to look for relaxation as compensation. You want to release tension or to relax, always trying to adjust your posture to find a better and more comfortable position. When it is not pleasant, you try this way and that way. This is a habit of avoiding – avoiding pain and discomfort and avoiding going through what is actually happening at the moment. We must make use of creative tension, allowing whatever is happening to carry on unimpeded. Give permission to yourself to experience such tension completely and see how the body actualizes its intelligence to deal with the situation. You are truly curious about this and therefore become totally awake and attentive.

It is very important also to see the way we hold our bodies, how we block ourselves and how we misuse our bodies. For the way the body is held determines where the blockages are: jaw, neck, head, shoulders, stomach, knees, ankles, etc. Feeling pain, deadness, coldness, shivering, or lifelessness indicates the holding points in the area. In addition to paying attention to that area, it is helpful to breathe into it and experience whatever feeling there is at that moment. This is not a technique but a way of helping yourself to get in touch with what lies beneath such feelings. Attention combined with breathing becomes more effective because of the conjunction of internal and external energies.

The body is the most accessible part of ourselves. It can be used as a vehicle for a journey through our lives at the levels of manifestation. When the body reveals and uncovers the deposited karma, we also find the mind operating and moving around the area in question. Certain parts of the body speak certain languages. The mind of the stomach says something, whilst the mind of the heart talks about something else, and the mind of the head is concerned with its own affairs. The term 'mind' used here refers to psychological conditioning and repressive feelings. In Buddhist terminology, the mind in this context is equivalent to body-consciousness, one of six forms of consciousness functioning within the human system. Because different areas of the body contain different conditionings and different feelings, so different languages are spoken. This is where, and how, conflict arises in life. Misunderstanding and lack of communication become inevitable. For instance, when the head dominates the genitals with its greed and compulsive desire, the heart condemns such behaviour and becomes frozen, cutting off all communications. As a result, the chest area is constricted and negative energy is locked up there. According to the language of the heart, it is a matter of protecting itself by contracting the muscles and withdrawing into its small world. It also covers itself with iron bands so that it will not be broken. In this way, the heart becomes painful; its longings and needs are obstructed and cannot be satisfied.

The heart wants to love, to be loved, to expand and to reach out, for it is too cold and frozen in its constricted world all the time. Consequently, ache, pain, tightness and sorrow occupy the heart, and therefore it cries for help. This is where the necessity for clearing up and cleaning out the blocked energies comes into being. The feeling tells us what is happening and we respond to it with caring and loving attention. Feeling is the language of the body and mind. If you want to understand what the body or mind is trying to convey to you, you need to watch the feeling at the point of contact. Then you will know exactly what it is talking about. Words that come with the mind or thought are misleading and very often distort reality. But feeling will never tell a lie about psychological facts in the body or mind. With clear understanding we can truly respond.

The Buddha emphasized the feelings, which traditionally-minded Buddhists tend to ignore. He said: 'Stop yourself at feeling'. It is quite clear that he instructed his monks and lay-followers to pay attention to feelings at every point of contact through the senses and with every movement of life. He does not encourage us to jump over into thinking, reasoning and intellectualization, which will lead to creation and the accumulation of karma. These reactions also produce words, and words are not the language of life but simply ideas, symbols created through tradition, culture, education and training. The language of life is feeling. You come to understand what your life is communicating to you when you attend to and observe feeling.

5.

NON-DWELLING MIND

Those who are aware always rise; they never sink down. Nor do they have a 'dwelling place'; they can *move*, from one thing to the other.

It is very hard for the mind not to dwell on anything. But because of wanting to – being conditioned to – find a dwelling place, the mind cannot avoid suffering and pain. So the mind has no choice . . . no choice in the way of being able to escape pain and suffering, because of that *heavy* condition of wanting to have a dwelling place. It has to be *somewhere*; it has to have *something* to abide in, otherwise it cannot feel secure, or safe.

But the essence of Vipassana practice is to have that quality of a *non-dwelling* mind. See how you become *fixed*, or *rigid* – with ideas, with principles, with rules. Or with the method, the technique, the way of life, the spiritual path. Then you become *attached*; *you identify yourself with something*. You are then fixed with your insight, you are fixed with your understanding, or you are fixed with your belief and your experiences.

All these places are dwelling places for the mind. When you are in that situation, how do you feel? Observe how you feel when you have this rigid inflexibility, not being able to bend –

when you think 'This must be like *this*, it cannot be otherwise'. You see how painful it will be, if you maintain that attitude.

Or you say, 'Meditation is like this' – either being silent, or making noises. If you have a fixed attitude towards one or the other, then you have a problem.

But the non-dwelling mind will say, 'You cannot expect anything to be anything; but you will have to meet whatever arises'. So when there is *complete openness* to whatever arises, your state of mind is very different from that of the fixed mind, which has certain ideas, certain attitudes, and certain expectations. It is not the way of pretending not to suffer; but there is no suffering, once you are in that state of mind of being open – not holding, not dwelling on any principle, or any idea, or any belief, or any tradition. Such a mind is so free. So free to move. And so free to respond, to be *sensitive* to what is happening around it. And such a mind is *intelligent*, and more *capable* of coping with situations. Once there is nothing behind, to direct the course of action, then the action is freely taken.

But how is it possible for the mind not to dwell on anything? It comes back to awareness. If we are in a constant state of awareness, the mind does not dwell on anything; it flows, it moves freely. You have to see that awareness is *always* flowing and moving . . . it does not *fix* itself on an object. It does not create any abiding point. It is like a bee going from flower to flower. This kind of awareness flows with *non-dwelling* mind. Non-dwelling mind is not created, but such mind comes to be naturally, when we are in that state of awareness.

In the case of suffering, it is hard sometimes to let go of the fact, even if we know that this fact must be eliminated. The mind clings to the fact of suffering and repeats to itself: 'I am hurt, I am hurt, I am hurt'. The mind cannot let go. Thus the mind clings to its dwelling place, to its own karma, and is not able to let itself be free from what it experiences.

It is ignorance that helps us to create the 'dwelling place'. We have to see how painful it is to dwell on something. Without this realization there is no possibility of becoming liberated by having non-dwelling mind. We have to learn to be free from what we know, from what we experience. With such freedom, we know more, we learn more.

There is no theory or philosophy which can perfectly contain truth. A philosophy or theory is only *one way* of explaining a subjective understanding or experience. But if we take the theory we build, or the philosophy we discover, to be the only way of life, then we create a dwelling place for the mind. Conversely, when you cease to cling to a particular theory or philosophy, new ones will become apparent and acceptable to you, because you are moving at a deeper level: you are occupying a wider space.

We have to see how the mind influences our lives, how we believe the mind. The mind is so plausible, so capable of creating things, of generating attraction, excitement. This in itself is not a bad thing, but it depends on how we relate to what the mind creates; we have the ability to learn to relate to the creations of mind, instead of trying to stop the mind from creating. In this way we make use of our inner resources and bring out our capacity to relate to the mind, and all the things it has created. The mind then becomes the entertainer. Many beautiful things are created. The mind is *wonderful*.

So long as the mind is conditioned, it cannot stop creating. Even what we call the 'conditioned state' (or the Buddhist term, *sankhara*) within us cannot really be eliminated so long as we have body and mind. But we can have liberation and freedom in relating to the *sankhara*, the conditioned state. The conditioned state still remains, but has no *compulsiveness*. We become more flexible in relating to the world. Coming to the world, we have to use our *sankharas*. We cannot get away from *sankhara* – you cannot use Nirvana to deal with the world. But because *sankhara* is now 'under control', and not a compulsion, it can be used; before, *it* was using *us*.

So then we can relate to the world, using certain conditions to meet with the world, without suffering ourselves. Otherwise, you may feel you must create a community away from the world. But the *need* to contact the world will remain. You cannot cut yourself off completely. The *need* for contact, the old *sankhara*, stays within us.

There is nothing wrong with having contact with the world. The world is a very good place for testing ourselves – to see whether we are really liberated, whether we are really free.

Awareness helps us to *move*, to flow, so that we do not remain static. Buddha said, 'Those who are aware always *move*, always move on. Always rise.' That kind of energy is life, the movement of life. In this way, we can find our home anywhere: wherever we are is home, we feel at home. You never feel a stranger, never feel alienated from any place, or from anybody. You meet your fellow beings anywhere: you have kinship everywhere. This is the freedom associated with the movement of life, with the non-dwelling mind.

In this way you will feel that you are open to many things, and many things will come to you: joy, clarity, tranquillity, as well as pain and tension. And there will be emptiness: the non-dwelling mind *is* emptiness. With this emptiness, there is no place to dwell in; there is only clear space of being. Here there is no centre, there is no *point* – no fixed place to be.

Awareness does not create any fixed point. It breaks the point. In meditation, sometimes you *want* to be one-pointed; you *want* to be united with something. In desiring concentration, you are asking the mind to create a dwelling place, a narrow space. But if you allow yourself to break out of that narrow space, that one-pointedness, you will *flow* and *fly* into the vast world, into vast space . . . infinity.

All this is within us. It is not imagination. You *can* learn to be free from dwelling place; to bend, to move from point to point, from one thing to the other, becoming a 'purpose-less' and 'point-less' person.

6.

THE FLOW OF LIFE

If we believe that silence is necessary for meditation, we are uncomfortable when the silence is interrupted. Why? Because of expectation. If you can listen to noises and silence equally with the right attitude, you will see no difference between them. In silence, if you listen carefully, you will hear many things coming up, talking to you, making comments. The right way of listening is a form of meditation. We should not expect meditation to be just sitting, or walking mindfully, or eating mindfully, or doing anything slowly and quietly. What we do is not really important; but the way we do it will determine our meditative, or non-meditative, state.

Sometimes people are attached to forms, to external ways of acting as a form of meditation or non-meditation. But when you are 'in a form', you are trying to shape yourself in a certain way without really having the meditative mind. But some people who are attached to form would say, 'No, if you don't sit properly, in the lotus position, having your back straight, and everything in the right form of sitting, then you are not meditating'. When you try to sit, or lie down, relaxing with clear awareness, with complete attentiveness to what is going on around you, or inside you, surely you are meditating? We have to grasp the essential simplicity of meditation. Meditation is here and now. With simple, clear awareness, you see, you hear and you know what is happening. You know not only what is the object of meditation 'out there', but what is going on 'in here' as well, and how this reacts to the object, to the things going on outside. You are in contact; you are in touch with what is happening.

Most of the time we are cut-off from contact or relationship with the things going on outside and inside us. The 'cutting off' is an aspect of exclusion, concentration, fixation, being closed-in. This is the opposite of being open. But if we look carefully, we can see that most of us are afraid of being open; afraid of seeing something which we do not expect to see, particularly if that thing is frightening, or unpleasant.

Anxiety is often caused by not being able to let go of the past; by expecting the same unpleasant thing to happen again. Meditation is the means of letting go of the past, or of living through the past if it has been dealt with. It will be dealt with at the moment it comes. That is why we talk of meditation as 'living in the present, living in the now, in every moment'. If, in every moment you are fully awake, you have fully alive awareness, what else do you want?

We may ask: 'How can we be awake all the time?'. We feel it is a burden to be awake. Many people feel that if you are always awake, you will not be happy. But that is conforming to the *idea of awareness*, which is entirely different from *being aware*. Surely when we try to make an effort to be aware, it becomes a burden. But it does not mean that *awareness* is a burden. It is *making the effort* that burdens us. So we ask, 'Do we really need to make an effort to be aware, or can we just be aware?' No real effort is needed to be aware. Making an effort actually brings about a dispersal of energy, partly because energy is directed to the action, to the act of making the effort; energy is also used in anxiety and tension when concentrating on the goal of awareness. Energy therefore flows in several directions. When this happens, you become tired and frustrated in the absence of success. If you do succeed in gaining awareness through effort, you feel very proud; but as soon as you congratulate yourself, awareness drops away, leaving you frustrated once again.

But if you treat this whole process as a game, you can laugh at it; you will never become a victim through losing awareness. You should never experience a sense of hopelessness: there is hope all the time; hope without putting your energy into hoping for anything. There is hope also in the sense that your being is flowing in its own direction without stopping and that many possibilities are open to you; you are in a constant state of flow.

We may flounder in both negative and positive things. You can understand the negative things easily; you cannot move on, you become very unhappy with what you cannot do – your failures, the obstacles, the barriers. But being held back by positive things is very hard to comprehend, because the sensations are pleasurable. That is the main obstacle preventing further movement.

Wisdom comes through suffering and frustration, but neither state should be sought out or created. The point is, we have to see whether we are flowing or whether we are stuck instead of *trying* to flow. If you try to flow, again you are conforming to the *idea of flowing*. Conformity is a bad thing to our way of thinking. You can see that you may not conform to many things in society, but you conform to many ideas inside yourself, and because of this you are not free. If you can see exactly how you conform, then you can resume the state of flowing again.

People say one meditates in order to gain peace and happiness. That is right, too, but not completely so. If you 'conform' to gaining peace and happiness, then you overlook suffering and frustration, or you suppress them because you do not want to deal with them. To meditate is to have 'peace', so you repeat that mantra again and again. But it becomes harder to meditate because we have set a goal for ourselves. When we set a goal, the ego is trying to achieve, which is very natural for the ego. We then blame ourselves, or blame the ego, for not achieving the goal which has been set. If we are arguing with ourselves, or conducting an enquiry on our lack of success, we are not looking at what is happening. This puts us farther away from reality, because we are not looking at what is 'now'. We are looking at something 'there', in the past or in the future; we are not looking at what is happening *at the moment*.

When you are sitting, and you make some movements, some gestures, are you aware of your movements in relation to your feelings, or ideas? Or when you make movements because you feel nervous, are you *aware* that you are nervous? So very often we miss the relationship between our movements and our feelings. Try to grasp the differences between concentration and awareness. Awareness is open to *what is happening*; it sees everything connected with what is happening. It only requires that we should *look*. If we look constantly, then we shall see. If we do not look, we shall not see. However, if you look by fixing your attention on only one point, then you will miss many other things. To meditate with that idea is to fix the mind on something. But we react against being fixed. We like to feel like we are doing something. That is the action of ego; ego must feel itself doing something. But Vipassana says, 'Look at ego, it wants to do something'. Then ego becomes the object of meditation. You *see* what is the desire of the ego.

So what actually *is* meditation? We have been talking about something for quite some time and still, perhaps, you are unsure of the idea of meditation. The key is not to have the idea; but rather to get into the *action* of being aware; being attentive; living fully with what is happening now; being in touch with it. It does not matter whether you call it meditation or not. Some people may be clever enough to find a clear definition of what meditation is, but it becomes a great barrier to meditating. Do you see why? Because we conform to the idea – to *that* idea particularly. And the way of meditation is to be free; not to conform. Definition becomes a narrow path for us to walk upon.

We take things for granted. We say we know. But as soon as we say this, we have formed a conclusion. This disinclines us to examine other people's conclusions and we argue with those who disagree with our concept of meditation.

Arguing is just another way of avoiding innovation. It comes of carrying the past with us. Carrying anything over from the past becomes a burden. In order to live fully in the present, we have to lay down that burden. And in order to lay down the burden, we have to know what things we carry with us.

Meditation brings about an awareness of what we are, how we do things, how we become – moment to moment. If you judge yourself, and decide that you are a bad person, you are not being objective. By blaming yourself, you are not looking at what is happening *now*. 'Bad' and 'good' are opinions. Who can really say, 'This is bad, absolutely bad' without having an *opinion* about the badness or the goodness?

You are relatively bad or relatively good. You may write books about ethics, or you may simply see what is really happening and also examine the concepts of good and bad; how useful they are, and how useless they are. Then you will *see* the usefulness and the uselessness of the concepts, and transcend them. No more duality; no dichotomy.

This is the meditative state – being in the state of accepting anything equally without taking sides or without identifying ourselves with this or that. *Identification* is a very subtle barrier to being real. We are not *real* because we are always identifying with something – with an image, with an impression of ourselves. So, you cannot be *real* because you are an *image*. You are an *impression* – a very tiny part of you.

Vipassana is not being fixed to certain aspects of your personality, but acknowledging that you can be dominated by them from time to time. However, the dominating factor is connected with many other things, so that you have to be open to look and to see more about yourself. Then you become more and more open to different levels, to different states of your consciousness, to different things connected with your being, or becoming. The main point in Vipassana is to *see*.

Seeing is the only aim, if you want an aim or a goal. But this goal cannot be created. You cannot produce seeing. But when you look, you see. Just as when you walk, you get somewhere. So, when you close your eyes, you close yourself. Without looking, you cannot see. Seeing is not very difficult, but you have to know *how* we see. You see with certain ideas, certain attitudes, certain conditions, or there is what might be called pure seeing – which is simply seeing, without any qualifications. Seeing *is* awareness itself. So awareness cannot be separate from seeing, or looking.

Seeing – real seeing – is a liberating factor; it is also a creative power. But we must not *try* to liberate ourselves, for in so doing we conform to the idea of liberation. We try to create liberation. This is different from the liberation which cannot be created. Thus, we can lose liberation, because anything created is subject to change. The thing which is not created is always there. It cannot be possessed, but it can be experienced. So with full awareness, we come to liberation. Liberation, means that we are free from the conditioning and from the conditioned consciousness, so that we come to pure, luminous unconditioned consciousness.

Vipassana is looking at what is *here*. The past becomes the object of awareness, of meditation. The past is now, and because the past is presenting itself now, it is in the present. If you try consciously to look back it becomes *recollection*. Some people translate the Pali term *Sati*, or awareness, as recollection. But recollection is always concerned with the past. *Sati* is an aspect of recalling the past, of meditating upon the past; but also of looking at the present. At the same time, it has the capacity to provide insights into the future. All this is included in the term, *sati*. Therefore, the object of awareness is here, at this moment. If you look for something, it is *not* applying awareness. Vipassana does not require looking *for*, or looking back, but looking *at* what is in front of us here. Awareness allows anything to come: things in the past, things in the future. Let them come, and simply *look*.

Is there anything beyond ego? Can we let go of ego and put our trust in the action of what transcends the ego – our inner being? This is difficult. We know that that being has knowledge, wisdom, intelligence; but how can it be released, and how can we put our trust in something we are finally unsure of? We must be careful not to play ego games; we must believe that awareness or insight knows best. Ego thinks: 'I might not be able to deal with my problems'. But that is merely ego fear, or anxiety. If we think that there is always ego, we block ourselves and are out of touch with reality. If you cannot feel safe without the ego; if you cannot put your trust in an inner being that you feel may not be there, what can you do? Do nothing. Just let the ego suffer, and then watch it. You will come to a point at which the ego cannot struggle anymore, and it stops. When the ego stops struggling, things become quite different, and quite simple. You are now completely alone. There is no one trying to dominate you, direct you, or tell you what to do, and what not to do. In Pali, there is one term translated in English as: having a second to be with; a second not in the time sense, but a second person: ego, conditioning. And if this person is with you, you are not free. But who is this first person? Some people call it 'inner being'; others call it 'supreme self'. The terminology is unimportant: what *is* important is to see that first person: when this is achieved, the second person drops away. At that moment, you are left alone, truly alone – whole, all one: alone. To be completely integrated is to exist without the subject-object relationship; you become unified with the now consciousness. Then, surely, there is complete freedom. There is no desire for anything. Everything is available.

7.
SELF-RELIANCE AND DEPENDENCE

One of the aspects of the Buddha's teachings is self-reliance. It is not generally emphasized, but it is a very essential aspect of living.

As we understand it, we should not rely on other people all the time. If you rely on other people in order to be happy and secure, you are destroying these people, or at least you are exploiting them. At the same time you neglect this essential aspect of self-reliance. As we can see from observing our practice of life and that of other people, there is a close connection between self-reliance and dependence. There is the story of a man who was sent by the king to investigate the teachings of different teachers and different cultures. When he came back, after many years, he gave a short report: carrot. People often stay with the superficial aspects of religion: like the carrot, the part of real value is buried from sight. People want to have things made easy for them, but in the fulfilment of this desire is dependence.

Dependence has been dominating our life since we were born. In childhood when we cannot help ourselves physically, we need to rely on other people to take care of us. As a result of this dependence we neglect the cultivation of self-reliance. Whenever we have difficulties, we always think of going back to our parents to ask them for assistance.

When we have relationships with friends, we also create this kind of emotional, and even physical, dependence. We depend on our friends in order to feel that we have someone who can comfort us or who can help us when we feel lonely or when we are in trouble. Loneliness is the enemy of self-reliance. It arises because of dependence. If you are not dependent, you do not feel lonely and you do not have the desire to dominate or control, to play certain games of relationship. The domineering person feels deeply lonely because the desire to dominate and control puts him in a situation of agony and despair. Such a person feels empty when this desire cannot be fulfilled.

We cannot fulfill all our desires. An old saying goes, 'Thousands of rivers flow to the sea, but the sea can never be full of water.' In the same way desires flow with our life but they cannot be always fulfilled. That is why we need freedom from desire. In religion we always talk about freedom from desire and we feel it is impossible to get rid of desire. Sometimes Buddhism uses a strong term to describe how to remove desire: destroy it! Buddhism uses strong words in order that we look into this matter of desire more seriously so that we shall not be enslaved by desire.

As long as there is no freedom, there is slavery. We are enslaved by our inner conditions, by our habits and patterns. We are slaves to ourselves.

What does it mean to be free from desire? Does it mean we must not have desire at all? Or does it mean that we have some control over desire? In a sense, it means we use desire for a constructive purpose and a creative way of living instead of being used by desire. But we cannot be satisfied with anything forever. That is why the search for gratification and satisfaction has no end. We become slaves if we search and search according to this driving force of desire. I understand the freedom from desire to mean *freedom from the compulsion of desire*.

When we are free from this compulsion in any aspect of life, we feel free to move and to act. We are not held back and we are

not pushed or pulled, but we flow according to our understanding. When we are free from compulsion, the general
natural desires will be used for sustaining life. Nobody will
reject the use of natural desires – the desire for food, water,
warm clothes, shelter, and so on. All these are essential. But
freedom from compulsiveness of desire is essential.

Let us look more closely into this matter of emotional self-
reliance. Can we feel emotionally secure, at home with
ourselves, firm and stable in our relationships, in our way of
living or with any work we do, in any situation we happen to be
in? Or are we emotionally disturbed, insecure, emotionally
lacking, always wanting? The want is the lack. When we want
more, it means we lack more. We feel we have nothing inside
us. There is emotional insecurity within, which means lack of
self-reliance. How do we depend on our environment, on
people around us? We have to observe all these relationships
and the conditions of life which we maintain. If you can
understand, you do not need external support. You can sit in
your room quietly, peacefully, without feeling lonely. When
you go out with your friends, you can appreciate being with
them, but it does not mean you depend on them. It does not
mean that you reject social contact, but you do not seek it out
continually.

If we depend on other people or social occasions in order to
feel happy, then there is something lacking in us, especially if
that tendency is very strong. If we simply want to appreciate
and understand different ways of living, that is another matter.
Self-reliance is not the same as negative detachment, a
neurotic avoidance of people. People who are negatively
detached are very self-conscious. They find it very difficult to
speak up, to talk or even to ask questions, because they think
they may hurt the other person, or that they will be considered
stupid. These reactions indicate a lack of self-reliance. If you
keep away from people, it does not mean you rely on yourself.
You keep away because of a fear of meeting people, because of
a fear of not being able to face whatever comes up. This
attitude of keeping away is not healthy to life. You create a very
small world for yourself. If you cannot meet the world, you put
yourself in a prison.

However, one can keep away from people in the sense of withdrawing for a constructive purpose; you can withdraw into a quiet place in order to look more deeply into yourself to see who you are in that quiet silent way of living. You can see whether you have certain reactions to the silent life, which is impossible if you live in a noisy world, surrounded by people. There must be a balance between keeping away from people and being with them. These are lessons to test us and show whether we are relying on ourselves or whether we are still looking for dependency, even unconsciously.

When we cannot rely on ourselves and on our own inner resources, we experience envy, jealousy, resentment, hatred. We feel jealous of other people because we feel that they have qualities that we lack. We then try to compete with them, which exacerbates the jealousy and envy. But if you accept yourself and rely on whatever you have and try to bring out your potentialities, your human resources, you take other people as the mirrors in which you see something lacking or something useful. The relationship then becomes one of liberation and mutual sharing. This is love. Love is giving and sharing and not taking. If we take, we do not love; and when we try to take, to hold on, there is dependency.

If our relationship is based on love and understanding and freedom – in the sense of being free to be ourselves, allowing the other person to be as he or she is – then it becomes a healthy one. Because you do not want anything, you can simply share what you have; you do not have to rely on someone else in order to be healthy or happy. There is no such thing in your mind. Then everybody is trying to contribute and love is flowing. When you contribute, you give. The flow of love stops the moment you want to hold on, to grasp, to possess. Possessiveness is the greatest enemy of freedom.

Can we really live our life without possessing things? Possessing means being attached to things. It is different from having things. We must satisfy our basic needs in life, however. We have things not through grasping, but with opening and letting ourselves be free. If we lose the things we have, we understand; they have gone. If we lose a person we like very much, we understand that that is the nature of things. Nothing can remain forever. At the moment we lose something, we understand, thus avoiding frustration and unhappiness. This does not mean that you will not feel sad about what is lost. You feel sad naturally, but you understand it. Sadness is a feeling arising because of mental contact with something we lose. When we see it as a feeling, we see it as a bubble which melts away. It does not remain there or become negative unless we form a negative attitude towards it.

How can we overcome envy, jealousy and resentment? We simply do not try. Any efforts will lead to suppression. Just accept that you are envious or jealous or resentful, and then look at how these feelings arose. How did you come to such feelings? How do you hold on to them? How do you allow them to dominate your life? Look at the structure of these emotions. When you do not have complete self-reliance, you have competition in life. You play the comparing game. It may give you a sense of pride, but very often it creates frustration and unhappiness. The comparing game brings about more competition in life. The more you compete with the others, the more envious, jealous or resentful you become.

Now turn to yourself; rely on yourself. Be the light unto yourself, the refuge unto yourself. This is essential, particularly at this emotional level. Because we are grown up, we think we can rely on ourselves, but emotionally we are more like children, always wanting comfort from somebody else. If we do not grow up emotionally, we cannot be happy, we cannot be free. We cannot be self-reliant. We are always trying to depend on something outside, looking for a father-figure, or a mother-figure, or an authority-figure here and there. But there is no authority unless we give authority to someone. Authority is only our creation. Everybody has a function, but it does not mean that they automatically have authority over us. When you are self-reliant you are not submissive in your relationships with people. Neither do you dominate: your relationship is equal. At the same time you respect other people for what they are, recognizing people according to their status and function, but this recognition does not bring about fear.

When you go to so-called gurus, do not give authority to

them, submitting yourself completely, receiving everything blindly without questioning or enquiring. This does not mean you should be arrogant. You accept people and respect them for what they are, but at the same time you exercise your intelligence, examining them, not accepting blindly what they say. What we understand is very clear to us. We see it. We are neither over-receptive nor over-rejecting. When we do not embrace extreme practices, we walk the middle path. Our lives are balanced. When we differ strongly with what someone says, we have to look into our reactions. Everyone has the freedom to speak and the freedom to pick up or to let go. When you see and feel something which is not right, you must speak your mind according to how you feel. This sharing helps each person to grow, to live in a peaceful way; it is an alternative to conflict in relationship. Mutual sharing does not destroy self-reliance; it does not bring about this dependence. All the troubles in life come from dependence and lack of self-reliance. Let us think about this.

We have to understand completely what dependence means. Holding on, grasping, possessing is dependence – like holding on to a good experience in meditation; you make yourself dependent on experience. When you cannot repeat it again, you are very unhappy and disappointed. That is because of dependence, not because of self-reliance. Self-reliance means approaching everything freshly all the time. We have what we need to deal with situations. We do not need to carry special equipment. It goes with us. It is there. When you need it, it appears. When you are in a difficult situation, if you are self-reliant, you are aware of everything; and you always have something coming up. You may ask if you have to depend on something coming up. The answer is, no: it is not a matter of depending on it. We may have an expectation that when we are in a difficult situation, something will come up; but then we become dependent. If, on the other hand, we do not have any kind of ideal expectation, if we let everything come by itself, we put our touchstones of reality into practice: awareness, alertness, clarity of mind. You use all these things and then surely something comes up. If it does not come up, it does not matter; you do not feel disappointed.

We may ask how we can know that we are really aware, for we may be deluding ourselves. When we are very aware, we do not have an idea of awareness at all. We do not know *what* awareness is, but only that it *is*. It is being in contact with something deeper within us. Self-reliance brings about the freedom to be. Humility and simplicity in living come when you are self-reliant; self-reliant – without grasping or depending; then love flows. Because of the flow of love you act, you give – your service, information, anything you have. You forgive other people for their wrongdoings towards you. The whole world is completely open and clear. You do not bury dislike or hatred or resentment, so there is no explosive strength of negativity. There is no conflict. At the moment you experience conflict, look at it. See it so that it will not dominate. It dissolves by itself. You have light, love and refuge when you rely on yourself; when you do not seek refuge outside of yourself and do not reject anything that may come from the outside to help you at a difficult time. But your refuge is principally within you; it is wherever you go. You do not have to build up a shrine-room or an ashram in order to have a refuge. You may need some kind of gathering, you may need some place for the purpose of doing things together in a group. But we have to understand that the real refuge is inside; it is self-reliance.

The Buddha made it very clear. Be your own refuge, be a light unto yourself, have the truth as your own refuge. Who else can be your refuge? Having cultivated yourself well, you will find the refuge, even if it is hard to do so. To be well-cultivated means to live through yourself, through the world, through experiences, experiencing all the levels of yourself: physical, emotional, mental, spiritual. Do not shut yourself off, but experience things in order to understand and learn to live with them in harmony and in peace. If you do not understand all these things, you cannot live in harmony with them; they become dominating factors in life. The physical body, the emotions or mind can dominate us if we do not understand them. When we understand them and live through their tricks, they cannot use their tricks with us anymore. You have your weapon, which is insight into their situations –

immediate understanding of what is happening. You can exercise your physical body, emotions, mind, spirituality, everything you have. There are no restrictions, no rules. We are free, in the sense of not being driven by our emotions, our physical and psychological needs. We are not pushed or pulled by all these things. We are free to be. Not just free from resentment, envy or jealousy or any other negative states, but *free to be*. When you can allow yourself to be, you can permit others to be as well.

8.

THIS MATTER OF FEAR

Fear is the big thing in life, particularly in this modern world. People feel very insecure; they have emotional and psychological problems. Young people suffer much more, or perhaps they are more open in their suffering than older people. There are so many things going on that they get confused. People who are not familiar with these rapid changes may have fear, anxiety and emotional tensions. Fear is connected with anxiety and guilt. Enlightened people always talk about the wise man being free from fear and bondage. As long as we are not free to cope with fear, we shall not be wise. Our knowledge will be of no help in our life-situations. Sometimes fear comes without reason – having a bath you may be overwhelmed by a strong sense of fear which you don't understand. People who meditate alone in a cave may have this strong feeling of fear. In our everyday life we are always afraid of being rejected by our friends or the people we meet. We want to have friends and we cling to the idea of maintaining friendships; therefore we cannot be real with the people we have relationships with.

People are also afraid of loving. They want to love their friends or children, but they are afraid of loving them. If you watch yourself carefully, you will see that this is a fact. You want to be loved, but you are afraid of loving. Some people find it difficult to use the word love; this word has different meanings and there is fear of misunderstanding. The Buddhist monks are not allowed to use the word love, because according to the monastic tradition the monks are not supposed to love in the sense of having emotional reactions or possessiveness, which is what people understand by the word love in a narrow sense. Instead, Buddhists use the word *metta*, translated as loving-kindness.

But love is still there as a deep and genuine feeling or as the truth. Whether you have *metta* or love, if you have it, it is there, whatever word you use. People may be afraid of love, because they are afraid of attachment. See how we narrow our boundaries, build up walls in order to have security and feel safe. Fear is underlying all these patterns of behaviour. Being narrow-minded, selfish, anything that makes us narrow, is the outcome of fear. You feel that if you are not selfish, somebody will get ahead of you; so you have to compete. In order to compete, you have to be selfish. You have to be violent and cruel in doing your business so that you can get ahead of others. Violence, cruelty, injustice in our society comes from this condition of fear which distorts our reality, our true living.

Fear is closely connected with sorrow. Sorrow is a matter of loneliness. Sorrow means the feeling of dryness and lifelessness you sometimes experience. At the moment you feel lifeless, you see that there is loss. We are afraid because we do not want to lose. Sorrow comes because of affection or desire, craving, clinging and emotional dependence. When we are emotionally dependent on external things or people for our happiness and security, we unconsciously create fear in ourselves. Sometimes people may turn to the idea of being independent. Externally they can depend on themselves; financially and physically, but emotionally there is a deep layer of dependency which causes fear and anxiety, so that one cannot feel at home with oneself or in any place.

All these things are connected with our false identity, which distorts the whole of life. That is why we miss our true being, our true self – in the Western sense. When you identify yourself with something which is not you, how can you be real? It is not possible. We identify ourselves with our character or status, our position or work, image, our impression about ourselves. So we are ignorant of what we are *really*. If we know what we truly are, there is no problem. You do not become victimized by the arising and the perceiving of anxiety or fear, because these things have been with us since we were born into this life. Due to the fact that all these things have been very familiar to our consciousness, we get caught up in them, allowing them to dominate our life. Some people may see their image in different ways. You may see yourself as a dominant type of person or as a submissive person or as a detached person. We can see that this is false. If we are just that, we are not whole; we are just parts. Reality is missing. The dominant factor is only one factor, one fact in our way of living. Sometimes we dominate, sometimes we do not; sometimes we are attached, sometimes we are detached. All these are just factors arising in life. It is a mistake to identify with them. But we have to see what the controlling factor is in our personality. What is it that makes us feel unhappy, that causes suffering in our life? We have to keep our attention on that pattern to see it, to attend to it without saying that this is 'me' or 'mine'. The removal of that obstacle will provide the way for the true being to emerge; but we have to see the obstacle instead of hunting for the true being. We must attend to our obstacles. When we do that, we do not need to do anything about our true being; it comes to us.

If a child is brought up in an atmosphere of acceptance, taking things as they come, seeing things as they are, his personality is healthy, and there is little fear or anxiety; they do not become dominating factors in his life. But if a child is brought up in an atmosphere of ambition, competition and rigid discipline, he will suffer from anxiety. When his environment is in contradiction with the way he was brought up, his security is threatened and that causes more anxiety. Anxiety leads to fear and because of fear we make mistakes and then we feel guilty. We are guilty about what we have done, but also about what we should or should not have done. But if you leave out this matter of "shouldism", you do not have guilt.

You can see that it is really illusion. Illusion and reality go hand in hand. When we are caught up in illusion, we cannot see reality. But when we see reality, illusion disappears; seeing light, darkness is no more. Guilt is a psychological conditioning and is connected with rules and precepts and ultimate authority. If you have a rule, you have a standard for yourself, and if you fail to live up to the rule, you create guilt; or when you break the rule, you have a sense of guilt.

In India there is a dialectical materialism called *lokayata* which attacks all religions very strongly, saying that all religions use certain holy words to threaten people, such as 'good' and 'evil', 'heaven' and 'hell'. But if we understand what we *mean* by good and evil, or by heaven and hell, then they do not become a problem in our life. There is nothing absolutely good and nothing absolutely bad. Heaven is not eternal and hell is not its opposite, but they are both experiences in life. We go up to heaven and down to hell. In our experiences, when we torment ourselves, when we experience our emotional difficulties, we are in hell. When we experience joy, peace and bliss, we go to heaven. This oscillation keeps us from becoming static and makes us able to learn more and more.

Human beings are flexible. That is why we have to take full responsibility for ourselves, because we can go down or we can go up depending on our understanding and action. What happens when we are completely free and liberated? We still communicate with the world and heaven and hell are still experienced through the senses. Sometimes we have unpleasant feelings, but everything is in control. We can cope with them without difficulty; we are no longer the victim of heaven-and-hell experiences. When you are liberated, though you still have unpleasant feelings and excitement, there is a balance of personality; of emotion and of feeling. Then personality becomes healthy. It is not a threatening factor and one is not bound to a certain thing or belief. The boundary which binds us to certain beliefs, ideas or patterns is broken.

Freedom comes, then, and is connected with our realization of ourselves, of our situations, in the sense of making ourselves real to ourselves and to others. When we see fear as the obstacle, we have to look at fear very closely when it arises.

What causes fear? Sometimes you think the other person may reject you if you speak your mind. But often the opposite thing happens. Constructive criticism is essential, but one must know how to give it. Perhaps we have been rejected in our life and we are afraid that history will repeat itself. Surely gentleness is essential in our communication, but it does not mean we must never use very strong words with other people. Some people sleep at a very deep level. We have to help them and use strong words, but with compassion, not with hatred or dislike or any other negative emotion.

Sometimes we hate ourselves. Why? Because we impose these 'shouldisms' on ourselves. When we cannot act according to our standards, we hate ourselves, reject ourselves, deepening the illusion and going further and further away from the realization of our true nature. Hatred can bring about more fear. When you hate yourself, you are afraid of looking into yourself, because you are afraid of seeing something unpleasant there. We cannot look deeper into the inner beauty; we are only in contact with the outer man. It is very easy for us to miss this inner reality, this truth. In Western terms, it is said that when you find yourself, your true being, you find God. God is what you truly are. Coming to that point there is no separation nor division; there is oneness of being. You feel identity, but it is identity with the whole. There is a kind of relationship because the one is the many. When you say you experience oneness, you also see the manyness. There is a kind of relationship which is not based on image. You are in union with the One Being; you are wholly with yourself, with your true being. Everything is included.

In Buddhism we talk about the extinction of all conditioned states. What is there, is called Nirvana; Nirvana is an extinguishing in which extinction becomes *being*; here the things which are extinguished are the manifestations, the unreality. There is also dying and there is rebirth. It takes place simultaneously. Buddhism refers to Nirvana as the process of extinction; coming to the Void. The Void is rebirth and the extinction of conditioned things is death. In Christianity they talk about death in Christ. It is the process of dying away from conditioned things, from imperfection. And when you come to 'Christ in us', it is rebirth, coming to your true being. In Islam there is the extinction in God. There is death. We should not be afraid of death. If we cannot die, we cannot be reborn. If we cannot die to the old, the new cannot come; the new cannot coexist with the old.

Once you have seen the truth, you have seen your own true being; then it takes some time for your external personality to actualize according to that seeing. We have to be patient. There is also the fear of losing what we have gained. Wanting to repeat an experience is also an obstacle. The experience we had may not come to our conscious level; but when it has been experienced, a radical change has taken place. It is working things out in our psyche, in our deeper mind, clearing up mental processes. But we still have to do something. It is like growing vegetables in our garden; we have to take care of them, nourish them, water them with care and love and understanding. Similarly we should not let our new experience be covered by the influences and distractions coming in our life.

The point is to see the false or idealized image which we identify with in order to discover our true nature. Idealization narrows our way of living, fixing us to a point so that we find it very difficult to move freely. When we are fixed to certain things, we feel uncomfortable when we hear people talking about ideas that conflict with our own. This is because we hold on to the belief or image we ourselves idealize. Without this image we can see what we are and stay with our true being. The effect of fear is then dispelled. You will avoid getting caught up in fear if you do not resist it and allow yourself to experience it fully. When you do not let yourself experience fear, then fear gets stronger and stronger. Once you allow yourself to experience it and see what fear is – without running away, postponing, avoiding, but going into it and seeing it for what it is – then you realize the truth of fear. If you feel like jumping because of fear, allow yourself to jump. Body and mind must co-operate. When you allow your body to shake fear out, you feel light and clear. When the body becomes clear, balanced, and integrated according to its structure, it provides a channel for the release of negative emotions such as fear, and for an unimpeded flow of life.

It is a matter of attitude. What happens spontaneously is something coming out of its own accord, but what happens intentionally comes from the ego, the self-concept, and at that level the will plays an active part. The will is a matter of ego; it is not you. We have free choice. It is not a matter of will because the will is closely connected with becoming. Nor is it connected with being. When someone simply wills something, he wants to become something or somebody; for example, becoming Bodhisatva in Mahayana Buddhism. He wills not to enter Nirvana until the last blade of grass becomes enlightened. But such will is false.

Real free choice comes together with *clear insight* into the situation at the moment and is *distinct* from personal will. So, freedom from will is wisdom in action.

9.
ON OPENING UP

When you see for yourself how insight is corrupted, you will understand the differences between pure insight and corrupted insight. I remember someone on a retreat remarking that I had been 'corrupted' by my experiences in California and was no longer following the line strictly. Expanding in new directions sometimes frightens people: they cling to the past.

But we have to grow and the growing has no end. You can see that the growing has to do with more eliminating, emitting, peeling off – like a snake. That is how snakes survive. Growing is the elimination of inhibitions, of unhealthy and destructive states: it is having more freedom, more liberation, more clarity, more openness, more flowing. We move towards fuller and fuller being.

This is why life becomes richer and richer – as long as we follow it. It doesn't become narrower, but wider, deeper, vaster. We have a certain foundation, but the foundation is just for us to step on, leading us on to other things.

That is why in Buddha's life story, they tell of the lotus coming up to support his foot; with each step he takes there was a lotus. In India the quality of the lotus is equated with the heart. The quality of the lotus is that it does not cling to anything; water stays on it but the lotus never becomes a container. Like the lotus, the heart is open and ready to receive the energy of the sun when it rises.

The more we eliminate our inhibitions, our constraints or obstructions, and the unhealthy, destructive qualities within our body and mind, the more good things flow in naturally. Then the natural flow of creative energy is coming. But because of obstacles, because of being constricted, the good things cannot come in.

But in order to flow we need awareness. With awareness, intelligence and wisdom result in flowing, in being, in expanding and growing, because we come across different things, some exciting, some terrifying and frightening. So there will be both sides of experience coming to us. But with awareness we are willing to live through, work through – not fighting, but just giving energy to enable the flow to continue. So then the growth cannot stop. It carries on so long as there is life. The way of growth is the way of eliminating all obstructions, allowing the seeds to grow. We have all the seeds inside to grow into being, completion and freedom. You become simple, and natural, you become what is at the moment. Then you are growing. In this way, you may say growing cannot stop; it goes on and on.

The more flow there is, the clearer awareness becomes. We are then open to contact; we watch and are constantly attentive. We must remain open without being occupied. If you are occupied by someone or something, by ideas, states, or experiences, the flow is impeded. So now you have the koan, the koan of flowing: 'How can you flow without being occupied?'

It is similar to the Buddhist precept of not killing: 'How can you eat meat without supporting the killers?' The Buddhist precept says no killing, but the Buddhists eat meat. How can you overcome your guilt? How can you solve this koan of not killing, but eating meat? Buddha says killing is one thing, and eating is another. There is the solution; although the Western mind finds it hard to think this way. You can apply this koan to other things in life, and then you can flow.

So it is very interesting to see how our mind obstructs the flow of life, creating fixations and obstructions. This is why insight can be corrupted easily. Insight can be put into a definite category, or content, and then it becomes ideas, fixations, conclusions, instead of immediate understanding of what *is*. The real meaning of insight is to understand anything immediately, and then just finish with it, not apply that understanding to other things. You cannot rely on anything, except a sensitive and alive awareness of the moment.

This can be a very frightening situation. Can we really throw ourselves into the moment without having the past to judge by, to help us to deal with what is in front of us? We are afraid – we must have something, some technique. That is our burden; it shows a lack of trust in our ability and our potentiality. But that potentiality is there; even if nothing comes up and you cannot cope with it, you accept it. That is another ability: to accept the fact that this time nothing comes up. You understand why nothing comes up. What happens is that you cannot be completely open; you are still expecting something to happen, something to come up. But that expectation creates a blockage. But if you remain open, then you know when something will flow through. That is Vipassana: by being completely nothing you can be anything and everything.

The real meaning of a koan is: the difficulty, the problem, something which is not clear, something which is indecisive. The way to deal with it is to look, and stay with it. When we see it clearly, totally, then the koan disappears. There is no koan. We can achieve *satori* anytime. *Satori* is growth; the problems and difficulties in life become the means for growth.

You experience a deeper satori in proportion to how deep the problem is. You become more awake, more alert, more understanding. If you just sit and are open to anything coming up, whether within you or around you, then you will learn to understand. The same applies to every situation in life: instead of becoming a subject at a given moment you identify yourself with watchfulness and awareness.

Suffering, for instance, is bad in the sense that the sufferer does not want to suffer. The sufferer cannot rid himself of suffering because he cannot solve the koan of suffering. For the sufferer himself *becomes* suffering. But when the sufferer becomes the object, then he can see himself, his real being, which, because it is so clear and pure, has no suffering whatsoever. This is how to deal with suffering. When we are caught up, particularly in the goal of removing suffering, we create problems for ourselves because we tense up. When we are confronted by a problem, the best way to deal with it is to *look.*

10.
BRIEF HISTORY OF VIPASSANA

Insight Meditation was discovered by the Buddha himself in his search for Truth. You might have read how the Buddha left the palace in which he lived to take up the life of a wandering ascetic. At that time people strongly believed in two main techniques of meditation. The first of these was strong concentration, which involved experiencing the different stages of meditative absorbtion, called *Jhāna*. The Buddha went to study with two famous teachers, and learned to master the technique, attaining the highest Jhānic state. But still his original aim, of finding the Truth or *Dhamma*, had not been fulfilled. He asked his teachers if they had anything more to offer him and they were honest in saying that they did not. He had done all they believed was required for the highest attainment in the spiritual life. So they asked him to stay with them and become a guru. But he answered that he had not reached his goal and was not ready to teach, and so left them.

The Buddha then came across the other form of meditative practice which was widely upheld in those days; self-mortification or self-torture. This was based on the belief that if you can torment the body, the self will die away, the ego will die.

This could be accomplished in different ways, including fasting or even lying on a bed of nails. The Buddha went through all the techniques until he came at last to fasting, which he practised intensely.

After months of fasting he came to a point of great exhaustion. He had no more energy to live. He was lying down half conscious under a banyan tree when a young cowherd discovered him. The young boy realized that the recluse must have been fasting for a long time because his body was very thin. The Buddha did not see the boy, but the boy was clever enough to help the recluse by giving him some milk. The Buddha was too weak to even open his mouth and the boy hesitated to touch him because he was of the untouchable caste. According to the Indian tradition, he knew that he must not touch the holy man, but he knew that the man would die unless he helped him to survive. He decided that even though it would be a sin to touch the man, he could save him and then ask him to forgive him.

Gradually, with the help of the milk, the Buddha felt better and he was finally able to move. He saw the boy sitting near him respectfully and he asked who he was. The boy told him that he was a cowherd and he told the recluse what he had done and asked for his forgiveness. The Buddha told the boy that he had done a good thing so there was nothing to forgive, and he went on to say that we are not good or bad because we are born in a high or low family, but because of our actions.

The Buddha stayed under the tree and in the evening he heard a song coming from the forest nearby. The song was sung by the girls who collected firewood in the forest and said that if the strings are very tight on a stringed instrument they will break when they are played; but if they are too loose, the instrument will not make the right sound. It has to be strung in the middle way – not too tight, not too loose. Through these words the Buddha saw the futility of extreme practices, and the danger of attachment to them. Now he would follow the middle path. He realized that he must discover the middle path himself. He went to the river and sat on the bank to meditate in order to find out what the middle way was.

It is told that the Buddha made a seat of grass under a bodhi tree and began to sit in meditation. Then a woman came by to offer him food for her good fortunes because she thought that the gods had come to her in this human form of the holy man sitting under the tree. So she offered him excellent food in forty-nine pieces on a beautiful tray. The recluse ate all the offering and then he prepared to begin his meditation without further need of nourishment. It was now sunset, and he determined not to move again until he had become enlightened.

Sometime after midnight he was very strongly tempted by Māra, the symbol of all obstructing forces. Māra's three daughters, Desire, Lust and Aversion, came to persuade Buddha to give up his practices and return to his palace where he would become king. But the Buddha was not swayed and this made Māra very angry, so he sent his armies by land and air to frighten the Buddha, who became afraid. He opened his eyes and raised his hand to ward off the attack. But then he realized that there was, in fact, nothing there. It had all been his own hallucinations.

So he continued his meditation, watching his mind until, at dawn, with the clear inner understanding of all phenomena, within him and without him, he attained to enlightenment and liberation. It was during this meditation that he discovered the method we call insight meditation. Insight meditation is based on constant, attentive awareness. Nowadays the word awareness is given various meanings, so that we should be clear what we mean by it. To be aware is to look attentively without applying knowledge or information; it means that we simply look with a quiet mind. If the mind is not quiet, then look at the mind being noisy. You can attend to anything going on in the body or the mind without making comments or applying knowledge, interpretation or explanation. The art of passive observation is not easy, but by so doing we are able to see that the mind can be emptied of its contents. We can then understand the way the mind works and can examine the contents of the mind. It is the way to meet everything fully with the whole being, with all the energy you have. The energy is not dissipated, and it can be directed into this channel of looking at what is going on, looking beyond the appearance. Looking beyond can become natural, when looking *at* becomes steady.

It is important to understand that we are paying attention, 'looking *at*', and not expecting, which is 'looking *for*'. If we look *for* something in our meditation, if we expect to achieve, then we may become disappointed. There will be clinging, energy will be dissipated and balance will be lost. It is essential to look attentively and silently in order to see clearly. The Buddha made it very clear in the *Satipatthana Sutra*, the Discourse on Mindfulness, that awareness is established just for intuitive understanding and awareness itself, not for anything more.

Intuitive insight is gradually developed along the way of awareness. We may see that in this way of practice there are three main factors: attention, awareness and watchfulness. These three words represent the method of insight. Insight is developed if we do this properly; in other words, if meditation is done in the right way.

The early stages of insight may be closely connected with the intellect because of the conflicts and knowledge we already have; but with insight we come to understand what we know. We not only know, we understand. Insight gradually becomes deeper, revealing the difference between insight itself and the function of intellect. The two are quite co-operative, even in deep meditation, but this co-operation may be different from what we may originally assume it to be. The intellect will become still and, therefore, receptive during the time that insight is operating. Then the intellect can pick up the signals given by the insight – words and concepts.

We want to allow our intellect to become quiet, not to be active all the time, because if it is unduly active we cannot come to the emptiness of the mind. We cannot come to the complete silence. When we reach the place of stillness, we can see without obstruction, and that seeing is insight. It is the meaning of the method.

To begin with we need to cultivate our attention and in developing attention we need some primary object to be a focus. We normally use the rising and falling of the breath as the preliminary object. We do not regulate the breath, just let it be as it is. Let the breath go in and out as naturally as possible without the mind interfering. When the breath goes in and out naturally, we can see the rising and falling. This is the first step for the mind – to see the nature of the rising and passing away in the physical sense of the breathing.

There are three aspects of anything which is going on: the rising, existing and falling away. In the case of breathing, we can say that there is a pausing of the breath which will lead us to a silence and it is possible for us to transcend the consciousness of the breathing. It seems like the breathing stops but actually that is not so. The breathing becomes very deep and even and we just breathe internally and do not feel the movement. Then we say that the breathing stops because we do not see the gentle movement. Another way to say it is that at that moment the breathing is not essential to us. The silence is more interesting and that is why we can transcend the consciousness of the breathing. In that case, you should not cling to the object. The preliminary object is something to start with.

We pay attention to the immediate object which is evident. In this way there is no set object. Everything that enters consciousness becomes the object for meditation. We identify with attention, awareness and watchfulness and the observer is not us. You are the observing and you observe the reactions of the observer. It is possible for both the body and mind to discharge when we begin to get into meditation. We just let them discharge but we have to know what is happening, knowing just for knowing's sake, not for doing anything. We become nothing and let awareness work. There will be a point when the whole action will operate, and intuitive wisdom will take over.

For instance, when you sit for long periods your legs will go to sleep; you will be concerned about this, but let them go to sleep. They want to. It is important for you to maintain the body in the upright and erect position. Sometimes the legs will 'wake up', but you should not worry about them too much. It is essential not to move because of pain or discomfort, because when you move you do not observe what is really going on in your mind. You just want the body to be comfortable. If we can bear to look constantly, we can see, we can know. We know what to do. You must not try to *do* first. You must *see* first.

When it is raining we can sit and let the rain pour down and just look at what is happening in our body and in our mind. We want to feel what our attitude is.

That is the simple way to do it. We should be simple. Otherwise we become involved in more and more difficulties. To be simple is not to conform, but to attend to what is happening. Do not look for a technique to help you get out of a situation. Put yourself into that situation completely. Without it, you cannot really learn.

Life is always open. We can say that in life there is always an open hand. It may not give you all the rewards you want, otherwise you would not learn. When you feel that there is something lacking, then you will look and learn. Life has both shallowness and depth; it has both good and bad things for us to go through. We have to go through all aspects of life. We should not expect anything but should take things as they are and as they come.

In this form of meditation we close the eyes. Keep the attention steady and take the rising and falling of the breathing as a focus. Before beginning, a bell is rung three times. This is another tradition in the East. You listen to the sound from beginning to end, following the sound, aware of the continuity of hearing.

When we begin to meditate we have fears and uncertainties. There is a story, told by Buddha to his disciples to help them in their practice, of a man who came across four poisonous snakes*. He was afraid and, trying to escape, ran away into a village expecting help. But there was nobody there so this caused him even more fear, and uncertainty. So he ran, till he came to a vast stretch of water. He did not know what to do because there was no boat to transport him to the other shore, and he became more frightened. Then he thought, why not make a raft? So he took some reeds and branches and assembled a raft and started out on his journey. Arriving on the other shore he abandoned his raft and at last was free to enjoy himself looking around at the new land.

It is the same with our meditation. At the beginning it may

* Symbolic of water, earth, fire and wind.

be like trying to escape from the four poisonous snakes. Sooner or later we shall come to a challenging situation, and in that situation we cannot rely on anything; nothing is available. But when we look into ourselves we can bring out everything we need: we can build our raft.

The Buddha told us also that this raft is for crossing over the sea of life, not for clinging to. If there is clinging, grasping, attachment, you may stay in the ocean, or you may even drown. Also, it cannot be carried with you when you set foot on the other shore, for then it becomes a burden. Any teaching is for helping us to flow, but not for grasping and holding on to, for then we become rigid and fixed and cannot move, cannot flow. We get stuck in the teaching process itself. The teaching is useful but we cannot fix ourselves to it. If you become fixed to the teaching you will become narrow minded. There is no openness, flexibility or adaptability. To move from one point to another, you must remain open. Then awareness becomes stronger. In Buddhism we call this self-reliance.

Some Questions and Answers

Question: I sometimes find myself in meditation doing a lot of swallowing. *Dhiravamsa:* Allow anything to happen. Allow it to be. There is a fluidity in the body that is one of the poisonous snakes. We do not run away from it but allow it to happen. If there is a tendency to swallow too much, enquire into it. It may be because you are feeling nervous and because the body is excited it produces more saliva. Sometimes we think too much and this can create this tendency to swallow. That is why I say we have to look into it. You can be aware of the action of bringing it up. That is what is meant by attending to what is happening.

Question: The pain in my left leg is getting worse and worse. Will it ever go away? *Dhiravamsa:* You have to see that you have the right position when you sit. Check your position. It is good then to allow it to go to sleep until it feels normal again. There is a point when it will come back. You should be patient enough to wait for that moment. If you sit for half an hour to forty-five minutes, that will be enough.

Question: What if your arm should rise during meditation? *Dhiravamsa:* You should allow it to rise and watch what is happening. It is an unconscious tendency to move the body and you have to attend to it. Furthermore, you should watch this tendency to raise the arm. Attend not only to the movement but also to the tendency. You will know what to do. Sometimes there is a habit of clearing the throat, for example, and people will clear their throats again and again without noticing. I tell them to watch the tendency to clear the throat. Anything coming into consciousness should not be ignored. Everything that happens is to be observed. We must see it for what it is and then let it go, not ignoring or avoiding but seeing it, observing it.

Question: During my meditation I heard a voice saying, 'My body is suffering but I am not suffering'. *Dhiravamsa:* Perhaps you have to attend to the idea that 'my' is different from 'I am'. It seems that you have two entities within you. Being free from pain is the tendency to avoid pain by giving you the idea that you are not the body. Some part of you is avoiding. You have to enquire why there are two entities. There may be a tendency to ignore, maybe to suppress pain.

Question: I have the tendency to become sleepy. *Dhiravamsa:* You have to understand how you come to be attached, to see the process of being attached. That way you do not turn away from yourself and then the attachment passes naturally. Sleepiness indicates a mental attitude as well as the need for sleep. When this comes up in your meditation, give up watching the breath and attend to the sleepiness in order to see if it is a physical need for a mental attitude.

Perhaps the first thing to see is what is going on within us, and then to see what we are not; then we will be able to see what we really are. Without seeing who you are not, it is impossible to see who you are. Looking into one's self may be a limited process to begin with, but when you can really look, then that looking becomes unlimited. You can see yourself in the unlimited sphere of life. It is a matter of seeing things as they are, having insight into reality. The alternative is to live blindly in a world limited by our conditioning, closed in by preconceived ideas, waiting for knowledge to be always interpreting for us. But sometimes we may glimpse that there is another way of understanding, and experiencing. We begin to *see*.

In order to see deeply and clearly there must be a constant state of enquiry. In the Zen tradition, it is said: 'The greater the doubt, the greater the *satori*'. This enquiry is done with a silent mind, in stillness, using a precise question and then forgetting the question. Do not look for the question. Become completely silent and let the answer come out.

During meditation you should keep the mind constantly alert. Acknowledge what comes without getting carried away by the happenings. Allow things to happen and leave them alone. They will not bother you. When you try to avoid what is happening you may meet resistance and then you may find yourself on a battlefield. You will spend your energy unnecessarily because energy will be absorbed in the fighting. Direct energy to observing, seeing things for what they are. Then insight becomes deep, and awareness will flow.

11.

SOME PRINCIPLES OF VIPASSANA

Awareness of the Body

First let us discuss the three main factors which are essential for insight development, as stated in the Buddha's discourse on the application of mindfulness. In the very beginning of his discourse he gave instruction to the monks to be in constant practice and constantly aware and have clarity of understanding of what was happening moment by moment.

The first principle is *perseverance*, perseverance in the sense of meditating or applying meditative principles to everything that comes into consciousness. In that sense the Pali word *atapi* is used, literally meaning burning things away. You might have heard of the man who practiced *tapa*, the very strong power of burning things away. This practice usually involves austerities.

The act of burning comes particularly in sitting. When you sit continuously, then you may have the sense of burning both psychologically and physically. Sometimes you will feel your head is on fire. Sometimes you find it difficult to sit because of strong sensations such as burning in your stomach or in your back. This burning is quite common in the Vipassana practice.

Another common sensation is itching and you may feel a tendency to scratch. Sometimes this is very strong. You might also feel something like insects or ants climbing over your scalp. We explain this as a cleansing off or burning away of tensions in the body, emotions, and mind. They have to come out through the body. People who have been thinking tensely about certain problems for some time, those who depend too much on an intellectual approach to life, usually have this burning sensation in the head.

This is what the Buddha meant when he spoke of burning things away. This has to be a constant process, but without the intention of burning. You do not have to do anything but sit, keep the mind alert and be aware of what is happening. Let everything happen as it wants to happen. This quality is concerned in a practical way with perseverance, or constant and continuous practice.

You can see that if you just practise meditation once in the morning and once in the evening there is no continuity. Perseverance is essential for any real effect. Brief daily meditation periods are not enough. We need a period of long, continuous practice such as an intensive retreat for ten days, two weeks, three weeks, six weeks or six months. Then you will feel energy everywhere in yourself instead of feeling the body simply as form or shape.

The second factor of Vipassana is *awareness* itself. In Pali it is called *Sati*. The Buddha gave advice to an old man who came to ask him about the practice. He was getting old and he wondered about a shortcut. People always want to find a shortcut. The Buddha said, 'Have awareness constantly and look at the world as emptiness.' This factor of awareness implies being constantly alert and attentive to anything – feelings, emotions, thoughts, environment, people, everything concerning life. This constant awareness is the main principle for the development of insight and for coming to liberation.

Liberation reached through insight is called freedom through intuitive wisdom. There are two ways of getting liberation. The first is going through mind-control in the tranquillity type of meditation. The second is through mindful

awareness, watching the mind. Mind-watching will lead to
liberation through intuitive wisdom. So insight is the way of
awareness.

The third factor of Vipassana is *clarity of knowing*. This
implies knowing totally, knowing without having knowledge
to interfere. The three things go together – perseverance, awareness, clear knowing and perseverance, particularly the last
two. Whenever there is awareness there is knowing. These two
cannot be separated, and they work very closely.

Awareness can shape one's way of life in the way of building
up the discipline of paying attention. If you are constantly
aware, you will be able to know. Then this becomes the natural
way of living, and if we keep these three factors in mind we will
not lose the spirit of meditation. When you come to something
which is unknown to you, there will be no frustration. If we
understand that whenever there is awareness, knowing arises,
then there is no doubt, no uncertainty. Doubt arises because
of not seeing clearly, not understanding thoroughly what is;
then we cannot make decisions. But coming to the point of
seeing directly by yourself, realizing the truth by seeing it face
to face, how can doubt arise? There is no doubt and you do not
need confirmation from anyone else because you are the
ultimate authority. There is no external authority apart from
yourself, the person who sees. If we need confirmation from
someone else it means that we do not see clearly. If you
experience it yourself, it is yours. When the mind is completely
clear it knows beyond doubt.

Keep these three factors in mind – the act of burning,
awareness and clearly seeing. Clarity of mind comes when we
are constantly attentive. We do not have to try to make it clear.
Just learn to be constantly aware, to be in touch with whatever
arises in every moment, right now. Sometimes you might have
a problem of doubt when you do not feel clear; but then you
must work on the doubt. You must keep full attention on that
area. The attention has the power to burn away doubt. If you
put your full energy on that area it is like the sun's rays on a
piece of tinder. In the same way, attention is energy when it
becomes focused.

From this discussion we will now move on to the subject of

the four categories of awareness. The first category is awareness of the body, including the body's activities and functions. The first bodily activity is awareness of breathing. In the practice of this awareness we must remember that we are not practising a breathing exercise. In sitting, we practise the exercise only of awareness. It is very essential to see how the breath comes in and goes out, how it arises and passes away, moment to moment. This is an essential quality of Vipassana. Everybody has to see the nature of arising and passing away. It is the nature of everything in the world. By seeing that we shall see the development and decay and impermanence of everything because nothing can remain forever. It has to fall. It shows the nature of transcience. There is a continuity of this arising and falling. We see only the continuity; that is why we see the sameness of things. We do not see the breaking up. If we see the breaking up, moment to moment, of any process or any object, then we will have no doubt about the nature of impermanence. Everything is in a constant state of change. Nothing is everlasting in the phenomenal world.

Also regarding the awareness of breathing, one has to see the appearing and disappearing. We must see the conditions of the breathing, why breathing goes on and on forever until we die. What is the reason for breathing? You have to *see*, for then you can see life. Life has attachment within itself, attachment to continuity, to existence and to the continuation of existence. Without that attachment life could not continue. Some people call breathing the life force. Buddhism does not use this phrase because there is another word for life force – *Jivitindriya*. This is the vitality of life which goes on as a form of energy. We have to see this underlying condition of constant breathing and its continuity. When you see the associative factors of breathing, you will see how many things are involved. Sensations are involved in breathing, as well as some movement of the body, and empty space; and sometimes we can see a stopping of the breathing. It means that on the surface there is no movement but there is a small movement going on in the depths of oneself which sustains life. In this way we refer to transcending bodily consciousness. Before you come to this point of complete stillness, there will be a time when you feel that the breathing is the only thing that exists in your consciousness. We say then that breathing has come to full consciousness.

The second category of bodily awareness relates to posture. Four main postures are involved – sitting, standing, walking and lying down. The important thing in regard to posture is to know clearly one's posture at each moment. So you become fully aware of your body in whatever position you are in. You will see whether or not it is balanced, or where there is tension. When you are lying down, be completely aware of the body lying. Be aware of sensations, of touching the surface below you; know clearly all aspects of that posture.

Sensations are always involved with the body because of touching. There is always contact. There is contact even with space and if you go outside there is contact with the wind, the sun, snow and the air. If we are very aware of how we put our body in the different positions and we know exactly how we do that, then we will be able to understand all our body's needs. This is because we are attending to every aspect of the body. We will know what posture the body likes and what gives the body pain. Many things go on with the body that we do not attend to and must learn to listen to. We have to look at all these things.

The next aspect of the body is bodily activities – gesturing, smiling, laughing, sneezing, coughing, hand movements and so on. When you are dressing you can look to see why you like to put on different clothes on different days. You can be aware of something in the mind that is connected with the body. When you are doing something you can see how you do it, the motive connected with it. You can see desire involved and you can see more than desire.

Eating, drinking, washing, waking up, going to bed, driving – all these activities can be attended to. For example, when you are eating you can attend to chewing, swallowing and you can feel the food in your stomach. Anything you do you will know clearly. You can think, perhaps, of 10,000 bodily activities. There must be full awareness of each one. You must know yourself clearly, whatever you are doing.

The next form of awareness is contemplation on the

cemetery. You may wonder why the Buddha suggested such a meditation. In the East when people die, their bodies are usually burned at cemeteries in the forest. When care is not taken with the bodies, they are sometimes left out in the open. Monks travelling through the forest sometimes come upon such bodies and they meditate on them. In their meditation, the monks would see the impermanence and decay of the bodies.

The main thing in this meditation is meditation on death, through the body. Death is concerned with life. If there is no death there is no life. If there is life, there is death. We cannot separate death from life.

So if we meditate on death, we shall be able to cope with death more easily when it comes. We shall not be afraid of dying. We shall see that the dying process is really going on in the body all the time; each physical process arises and passes away. But there is also continuity. So death becomes a condition of birth. That is why we have constant rebirth. We are born and die moment to moment. We have to remind ourselves of this.

You may experience death in your body. You may experience it in your feelings. That is the moment to meditate on that feeling, to be fully aware of feeling dead. Feel it more. Do not avoid it. Go into it. Perhaps you will come into contact with something more meaningful which will give you courage. This meditation is most beneficial.

There is one more thing to mention in relation to bodily awareness – that is, to look at the different parts of the body. Starting from the soles of the feet up to the crown of the head. How many parts are there? The Buddha has analyzed them into thirty-two parts. When you are sitting in the meditation position it is more beneficial to begin at the top of your head and move down. You can feel your hair at the top and then come down slowly, feeling every part of the head, the cells, the skin, your ears. See how you feel, look at your sensations. Look at your eyebrows, your nose and eyes, your chin – down to your feet. Very slowly, try to feel, stay there. Ask yourself, 'Is this part dead or alive?' Pay more attention to the areas you do not feel. Stay with them longer. You will learn a lot about the body.

Buddhism talks about four elements of the body in the symbolic forms of earth, water, fire and wind. That is extension, cohesion, temperature and motion or vibration. These four elements are the main elements operating in the body. That is why sometimes we feel expansion or extension of the body. Sometimes we feel lightness or we may feel that the body is completely unified in every part of itself – a kind of cohesiveness where there is space in each part of the body. You might feel the heat and you might feel the wind, the gas and the internal motion going on. These things will come into the field of awareness when awareness becomes broader and more complete. Then we can see our bodies clearly.

In a practical way we practise breathing awareness. Through the breathing we are in touch with our bodies. Walking meditation is very important for feeling the body when it is involved with movements. Occasionally you may want to meditate on the thirty-two parts of the body without trying to remember the different names, just go into it by yourself and see how many parts of the body you can see, both inside and outside, the skin and the organs – everything, both liquid and solid. See how you feel when you see each part. See how you feel about your body.

If you are aware of bodily activities it will also help you to meditate. Bodily actions are so obvious that we often miss them. Through these activities you can see your mind: bodily actions become a mirror in which the mind reflects itself. The body cannot function on its own. It functions together with the mind. The mind cannot function on its own either. It has to function with the body. They are interdependent. That is why if we start with the obvious – the body activities – we can see the many things involved with each activity, with anything we express, anything we manifest in the world. So we can see our awareness grow bigger and bigger because of our activities.

There is no limit for awareness. It can go anywhere. It can go beyond our activities. The point is to make use of it.

Awareness of Feelings and Sensations

There are two Pali terms involved with Vipassana practice. The first is *sati*, meaning clear awareness. It evokes the qualities of awakeness and alertness. The other Pali term is *anupassana*, meaning watching, looking or gazing, or paying continual attention to what is going on – *bare attention*. Both factors have to be established for their own sake, not for anything else. There is no purpose in developing awareness except for awareness itself. There is also a quality of independence involved, not depending on anything in order to be aware. In gaining awareness we are learning to be more independent – more and more ourselves, being free from conditioning.

Awareness is closely connected with insight. Insight comes at the moment awareness is present. Awareness is always in the here and now. We learn to get into contact with it and there are different objects that help us to get into contact with awareness, and to make use of it more and more.

In the Vipassana system, we have to *know*. At the moment of contacting feeling or sensation, the knowing must be there. The Buddha used to say, 'Stop yourself at the feeling'. He did not mean to stop the feeling. He meant to stop and *look at* the feeling. If we can stop and look, then our perception will be much purer because we perceive according to how we feel.

Most of the time we overlook our feelings. We jump into thinking, reasoning, forming opinions quickly. We suppress or overlook the feeling. That is why if a child is taught not to express his feelings, he will find it very difficult to be real when he grows up. He will have conflict inside because of that suppression of feeling. It is not wise to teach people to overlook their feelings.

Sometimes when we are grown up we have difficulty in expressing our feelings because of our upbringing. It is essential to feel what we feel and to sense what we sense, to experience what we experience. Do not turn away even if it is unpleasant. Stay with it, go into it, experience it as fully as possible. Then there is no postponement, no avoidance, no suppression. Everything is open and real.

The way of meditation is learning to be real. We have to know, too, how we become unreal. If we conform to an *idea* of being real, it will be much harder and also distorting. Being real will come to be when we understand how we become

SOME PRINCIPLES OF VIPASSANA   105

unreal. Feelings can tell us. These feelings we have are a reactive process between the senses and objects. This reactive process is going on all the time.

There is another kind of feeling which is much deeper and is not a reactive process. We may call it intuitive feeling, the feeling coming up from the depth of ourselves. You can always trust this feeling. It can never tell a lie. This feeling has insight associated with it. Sometimes spontaneously when you come across someone you have never seen before, if you are really aware of yourself, you will see that that feeling comes first before everything else, before the reactive process. The feeling will tell you about the person; it will give you the whole picture of the person.

An awareness of feelings both at the reactive and at the intuitive levels is essential for our growth and development. In the practice of Vipassana, when we have a feeling of discomfort we do not try to change our posture but look at that feeling first. Stay with the feeling and see what is wrong and how the feeling arises. You investigate your body, your posture and the sensation of discomfort which has arisen. After seeing it for what it is, you will know what to do; you will have insight into the situation of discomfort. Then you can take appropriate action according to how you feel and how you see at that moment. You allow yourself to act according to your immediate insight into your situation. Then you will begin to react less and less and to act more and more because you *see*.

Grief is a mental feeling and when it arises we must go into the whole structure of that feeling. Usually we try to avoid it, but we must allow ourselves to experience grief, see what it contains, see whether there is any connection between the grief and some other things in our lives. Then you are purifying your feelings by living through them. Let them come to full consciousness and let them express themselves, for then we neither suppress nor control. We do not try to express but simply allow the feeling to express itself. We have to trust our wisdom, and the wisdom of the body and the feelings. These things know what to do and how to express themselves. We stay with full awareness and do not turn away from our feelings.

Gradually, you will transcend all kinds of feelings and be able to accept them for what they are. By accepting our feelings we are not tormented or overwhelmed by them. In this way we become free in relation to any feeling, but we will not be free unless we go through and experience. Freedom comes in the relationship because of understanding and acceptance. If we accept things for what they are, accept people for what they are, we do not torment ourselves. We torment ourselves because we hold on to certain ideas or certain standards and we want to fit everything into our preconceived patterns. When things do not go as we think they *should* go, then we suffer. Thus, we really create our own suffering, not the object. We must always come back to ourselves to see how we create problems, difficulties and suffering. These then become the object of awareness.

When we become more and more aware of how we do things, how we manage ourselves, then we have more power to deal with our situation. We will have more strength, more clarity, clearer awareness, deeper understanding. Then everything is moving forward, moving deeper into our being.

Feeling is essential to seeing these things. If you do not feel, especially mentally, you will become paralyzed. When you meditate and you lose your feelings, you must then watch, watch this inner deadness, this paralysis. Look at that feeling and see what is happening in the body and the mind. There is then a possibility of finding a new feeling, possibly of an explosive kind.

In meditation we do not have to look for an object. Objects always come to us. Just sit there and do nothing, remain aware and watch. You do not have to look for something to come; you do not have to look for experience. Anything can come to you because you are open to whatever comes. Stay with openness, awareness, and attention. It is simple. You do not have to hold on to anything. You do not have to hold on to the object. When your awareness is cut off by distraction, when it is lost, pick it up. It is there. It can never be lost forever. We have to learn to pick up awareness. It is a matter of being able to catch the immediate present. This ability is a creative action.

Awareness of Mind and its States

The third principle of Vipassana meditation is called *cittanu-passana*, attentive and simple awareness of mind and mental states, including emotions. The word *citta* in Buddha-Dharma has a wide meaning. It also means consciousness. Sometimes we use both mind and consciousness as a translation of the Pali term *citta*, but it literally means thinking, accumulating and creating wonderous things, creating wonders. *Citta* manifests itself in everything wonderful in the world created by mind. You may have a scientific mind, a legal mind, a religious mind or artistic mind – that is *citta*.

The objective of Vipassana is to see and understand how the mind functions. This is the main target of Vipassana: to be able to see the mind, its state and its conditions. The mind has many properties, many possessions. We have to understand them all. It is not a matter of mind-*control* but of mind-*watching*. This mind-watching is an essential aspect of Vipassana meditation.

If we understand the word *citta* as mind and consciousness, we can see that it becomes the subject most of the time. The mind becomes the subject in the way of thinking, imagining, remembering and accumulating, speculating, forming ideas. That is why in the Dharma we do not believe in the self. What we call 'self' is a state of subjective consciousness. At any particular moment one may be in such a state of consciousness, but there are many states of consciousness. They arise one after another. The continual rising-up of different states of consciousness gives us the feeling of self-sameness, for then we identify ourselves with that feeling, creating a fixed identity to hold on to. We can look at consciousness as the subject of knowing. To be conscious is to know.

The mind's first function is to know, to perceive an object. In perception we have the sense faculties and the corresponding objects. As soon as the sense faculty comes into contact with a corresponding object, consciousness arises – knowing the presence of the sense faculty and the object. The first knowing of that is consciousness or *citta*. The presence of the three things – sense faculty, corresponding object and consciousness

– gives rise to contact or impression. Surely consciousness is always present when there is contact with senses and objects. If we observe how we perceive, how we hear, smell, taste, touch or how we think, then we will understand the function of the mind, the presence of consciousness. The mind cannot function without the body; the mental processes cannot function without the physical processes. The mind has to function together with the body. The sense faculties belong to the body and consciousness belongs to the mind.

If you are very aware of the sense faculties, how they operate, meditation can go on in your life all the time. Be aware of your touch, see what comes first. When you look at trees, buildings, people, see how you perceive. Then we see that *citta* does not only mean mind but also includes the contents of each consciousness. By understanding consciousness we understand the content or state of consciousness. Consciousness cannot arise without a state or a content. So we cannot really separate consciousness from its state. We have to see what the state is that arises with consciousness. Consciousness arises with greed or lust, desire, hatred, resentment, confusion, understanding, compassion and many other states. If you watch your mind in this way you will understand it better. Anytime you are conscious of an object and you see the content of your consciousness, then you understand it more deeply.

There is a general observation I would like to make. If you go along with observing the mind or consciousness, particularly in meditation, you will see what the state of consciousness is. You have clarity, wakefulness, reflection, investigation, looking at the details of the process with clarity of mind, seeing everything coming up one after another; you have joy, rapture, inner stability. It is important to know clearly each state which arises with each consciousness. If the mind is distracted or disturbed, you will know it for what it is. If the mind becomes transformed, know it for what it is at that moment. Just know it. Do not identify with any state but know each one for what it is. At that point you will not have a strong image of yourself; you will experience that state, rather than becoming it. Each state that arises – see it for what it is.

As I have said, emotions are included in this category. In the Buddha-Dharma, emotions are states of consciousness, mental states. Another word to use for emotions is content of mind: anger, sloth, torpor, anxiety, aggressiveness, restlessness, worry – all these are contents of mind, mental states. That is why in the Dharma there is no specific term for emotions. There is a term for feeling, but feeling is not emotion. Feeling is very weak compared with emotion. Feeling is just sensation, a feeble form of emotion.

Love in general is an emotion. It is a mental state. It is one of fifty-two mental states in the Dharma. In those fifty-two states the word emotion is included. Even the state of equanimity is included as a mental state. We often think of equanimity as an attitude, but it is actually a mental state. It is a state of balanced emotion.

In the Buddha's discourse on *cittanupassana* he also referred to seeing the mind when it is liberated – freedom of mind. Sariputta gave four characteristics of freedom. The first one of these is immeasurability. Freedom cannot be measured. When you come to that feeling, you cannot see how deep it is or how high it is. It seems to encompass all dimensions. The second characteristic is no-thingness. When you are really free there is nothing you can say. You do not feel 'I am free'. There is simply the state of being free. Nothing can be grasped and nothing can be said about it. The third characteristic is emptiness, voidness. It is empty of content, empty of substance, empty of emptiness. There is a sense that nothing is lacking. It is full but not full in the sense of being full of things – full in the sense of just being. You are fully being. The last characteristic is signlessness. There is no sign. You travel without signposts. Nothing is significant, nothing gives direction, no label or word or symbol is there.

Soon after his enlightenment the Buddha said, 'My mind has reached the unconditioned state.' If the unconditioned state of mind exists, there is liberation. Surely if the Buddha experienced this state it is possible for any one of us to attain this. In the unconditioned mind we are full of love because there is no conditioning. We can truly love without conditions. When we are in the conditioned mind, we can only love with certain conditions.

The way of insight meditation is the way of deconditioning ourselves by learning about our conditions and going through our conditioning. This conditioning includes everything at the cultural, educational and religious levels, as well as that which is part of our personality. The latter is referred to as our karma. That conditioning is called *sankhara*, the conditioning which comes with us when we are born. That conditioning has to come to an end. We have to unburden ourselves, lay down our burdens. Meditation is a means of ending karma. We have to see our karma and go through it. Any karma we have performed will have to give a result. You cannot avoid it. You can go to the sea, to the mountains, to the valley, you can hide anywhere but you cannot elude your karma. If we do not reap the result of our karma in our lives it will come to us in meditation so that we can experience it. That is why it is important to experience whatever comes at the moment. Be open to whatever appears. Do not let the right moment pass by. Be in the right moment. If you are actually in any moment, it is right.

12.

DIGGING AN ANT-HILL

The title of this chapter comes from one of the middle-length
sayings of the Buddha. Many of these Pali suttas are fundamental to the Buddha's teaching, particularly in relation to
Vipassana meditation.

It is very important when reading or listening to let the body
and mind relax, and not to try too hard to understand –
because sometimes the effort to understand can block the flow
of energy, and therefore the understanding. If we allow
ourselves to flow with what is being said, just dancing with it,
then we shall find it easier. Relaxation of the body and mind is
the basis of understanding when you listen; you may find you
receive flashes of insight into what is being said, although the
words may mean little to you. It is the contact with the energy
coming with the words that is important. So we can listen
passively at the ego/personality level but actively at the
awareness or energy level; then we begin to experience the
flow of life. Life is always in movement, always in contact:
there is no moment when there is no contact; whether it is with
sensations, the body, form, with thoughts, emptiness or
nothingness, life is always moving; there is always movement,

and we are moving with it. If we are sitting still in meditation there is still movement inside. Even in stillness you can feel a very deep and gentle movement – that is life.

I see few differences between life in the world and the meditative life. It all depends on our state of mind and the attitude we adopt in our lives. If we are in the meditative state of mind it does not matter what we do; whether we are dancing, eating, talking or drinking, it is the state of mind that indicates the way of being.

Often, when people come to meditation, they think about form too much; they believe there is a certain way of meditating. I do not deny that form is important; but form presents itself when we are in the meditative state. The meditative state does not imply fixation on one object; it must not be confused with concentration. When you are in the meditative state you are in touch with everything. You are not fixed to any particular thing, or state, or experience, or form. You are moving, and flowing, without being restless, without being carried away; this is the meditative state.

In his discourse the Buddha explains the story of the ant-hill to the monk Kumarakassapa. One night a deity appeared to Kumarakassapa and told him the story while he was meditating. The Deva said, 'Bikkhu! Bikkhu! Once there was an ant-hill which smoked at night and blazed up during the day. Also there was a Brahmin and a monk; and the Brahmin spoke to the monk, saying: "Wise man! dig the ant-hill, go and fetch your spade." So the wise man started to dig the ant-hill with his spade and presently he found a large iron bolt. So he looked at the Brahmin hesitantly, not knowing what to do. The Brahmin said, "Let it out! Carry on digging with your spade." So he carried on digging and then he found a frog, a huge king frog. He was startled so he looked up at the Brahmin for guidance. "Carry on digging! Let the frog go! Let it out of the ant-hill." So he let it out and carried on digging and then he came to a forked road, down there in the ant-hill. So he stopped digging and looked up at the Brahmin, full of doubt and confusion. "Let it out!" said the Brahmin. "Carry on digging!" The next thing he found in the ant-hill was a turtle; again the Brahmin had the same instructions for him: "Carry on, dig on! Let the turtle out!" So he carried on and he found a strainer. He did not know what to do this time either, so he just carried on and the Brahmin was at his side as usual, always available to give advice whenever there was any doubt or perplexity. The last thing he found at the bottom of the ant-hill was a cobra. The cobra was very large and powerful, and it rose up in the hole he had dug, swaying from side to side. The monk was scared. He looked up at the Brahmin, and the Brahmin said, "Do nothing! Let the serpent be! Now do reverence to it!"

The Bikkhu was perplexed as to the meaning of this story, so he went to the Buddha, and the Buddha told him what each part of the story meant.

The ant-hill is a synonym for the body, the physical system, with all its bones and flesh and physical energies. Like the body the ant-hill perishes, it cannot last very long. The body can be a channel for the flow of energy or it can be a container. If we allow it to be a container, we will hoard up garbage – that is to say, negative energy and destructive states of mind, which are buried in certain parts of the body. Hindu people talk about chakras; in the West we talk about the centres of energy; in psychology we call them holding points or blockages.

We can be blocked in the forehead, in the throat or mouth, in the chest, solar plexis or stomach, in the belly or the pelvic area, the genitals, in the thighs, knees or feet: all these areas can become containers for negative energies. Negative reactions like anger, hatred, hostility, and irritation, will be kept in the body so that we feel heavy, dull, blocked; we do not flow. The body needs to be like a baby's body. Babies have perfect posture – the back is completely straight without any effort, it's natural. We all started off like this, but gradually we have lost our structural integration, through what we have done to our bodies both from the outside and from the inside. Internally we fill our bodies with repressed emotions and feelings, causing tensions, cramps, and blockages; externally, we comfort ourselves, pandering to our internal confusion by assuming unnatural postures and eating unsuitable food and so on. We have to re-educate our bodies and try to rediscover their original sensitivity by cleansing them of their accumulation of obstructions.

In meditation we emphasize the posture, because it is essential for the meditative state to arise. When the posture is correct the meditative state arises naturally, for the body becomes a channel for an unobstructed flow of energy. When we breathe we take in not only air but energy as well, the energy that comes from the environment, and then we breathe out what is not desirable. The body is telling us the truth; that is, the filling and emptying, or opening and closing. This is the rhythm of life that goes on as long as we live.

The second meaning of the ant-hill concerns its becoming smoke at night and fire during the day. Smoke means thought, thinking at night, pondering, perhaps anxiously, as smoke is turbulent and cloudy. In the daytime all these things are put into action; the fire is activity. The Brahmin means the Buddha, or Buddha-nature, the natural understanding within us that is always available to tell us what to do and what not to do. The wise one or clever one in the story is the student of the Dharma who is learning to find the truth, to find himself. The spade is intuitive wisdom and the act of digging is putting energy into work – letting energy flow. With these things we go into the process of digging.

The first thing the monk found was the bolt. The bolt is ignorance – not knowing yourself. Ignorance in Buddhist teaching is the passion of ignoring – the absence of awareness. At the moment of absence of awareness we lose touch with reality of fact, with what is happening, and at that moment we invite ignorance.

Why do we cause ourselves pain and suffering in our lives? Why do we go into situations where we hurt ourselves and other people? The answer is ignorance. If we knew what would be the consequence of our actions we would see through them and we would not put ourselves in such situations. But we always do; in life we cause Karma to ourselves and to other people. That is because we have not cleansed the negative Karma from our bodies and minds. This destructive energy of bad Karma is always attaching itself to something similar. The energy that we have brings us into contact with the same type of energy in the outside world. If we can clean out our Karma, then we will not be led into any negative or destructive situations; we just flow with life.

This does not mean that we should avoid pain or difficult situations. We must learn to look into such situations with awareness, without being victimized: see how the situation has arisen, and thus become cleansed by it. That is why the Brahmin said, 'Let it out!'.

Ignorance is flowing out constantly through our actions and thoughts. To meditate is to be aware of how we act, not only of *what* we do but *how* we do it; the words we use and how we speak, what we think and how we think about things: meditation is a full-time job, twenty-four hours a day! If you are in touch with everything you come into contact with during your life, then you know how you react; you understand because of observing every contact that you make; that is the beginning and end of meditation. The awareness is there at the point of contact, and there meditation begins to flow with life. In this way we can begin to eliminate ignorance by being aware, so that we throw light on our actions and thoughts and the darkness gradually disappears; we become clear and light, which is natural. The process is gradual, although we may experience flashes of insight, like flashes of lightning when we see into various things; but we do not hold on to these things, we do not accumulate them. We only allow. In a similar way we may reach a point of exploding, like thunder; but whatever it is that is there, we let it arise. All these things are there, available; but we are not the owners.

In Buddhism, ignorance is described as not knowing the four noble truths. In life the truths are very simple. You do not have to think about theory – think about the facts in your life. If we see something happening in us or around us, it is *Dukkha*; whether it is painful or pleasurable, it is *Dukkha*. *Dukkha* feels like the duality of things; we have dualistic experiences – the two sides of one coin, meaning the experiences of life.

The second truth asks: 'How does this situation arise?' The third says, 'Ah! It has also this nature of ceasing, it will not stay forever.' Then the question comes: 'What is the way?' 'How can we put an end to *Dukkha*?'. That is the fourth truth. The way of Vipassana is that you meditate on these four noble truths in everyday life – not only in sitting meditation.

The second symbol is the frog. The frog means anger. The anger is blocking the flow of love. Whenever you feel angry, you cannot feel love. Anger is an emotional reaction which is normal to human beings; we all get angry, and anger is so common in life that we have to deal with it constantly. There is a short story about a demon who ate a certain diet and that diet was anger. He could find his food anywhere in the world as people get angry everywhere – so he was very well fed! One day he said to himself: 'I would like to try the anger of the Devas in heaven and see how it tastes!' So he went up to the heaven of the thirty-three deities, which is headed by Indra. When he arrived there Indra was not in his palace, which was very beautiful; so he went and sat down and made himself at home in Indra's throne, and waited for the deities to come in. Presently a few deities came in and saw the demon sitting on Indra's throne. 'Demon! How *dare* you come and sit on the throne of our king!', they shouted at him. After a while a few more deities came in and produced the same reaction – they threw all their anger at the demon, who just kept on eating. Eventually all the deities were in the throne room – giving him all their anger. The demon just kept on eating and the more he ate the more smoke he gave out, until the whole room was full of it, and the deities began to lose all their radiance.

Then Indra returned and he was very friendly; he walked in with a big smile and went up to the demon and said to him: 'Hello, my friend! How nice to see you here!' All this came from Indra's heart, he was not pretending. And the demon was afraid. Meanwhile, Indra was talking about entertaining the demon to the other deities, because he was so pleased to have him in the palace. He described the two different drinks he had in his heaven. One is called Amarita and the other Soma. Amarita bestows immortality and Soma is a very intoxicating drink.

'Which one would you like, demon?' Indra asked. But the demon was afraid, full of fear; he was sinking down, down, until he disappeared into the throne; he never returned, so Indra never got the chance to entertain him!

This story tells us that there are two ways of working with anger; the first is to get in touch with it in a gentle way so that we do not reinforce it. We just stay with it and experience it, letting it act out through our bodies and minds. This way we let it come into full consciousness, so we stay with full awareness of it, and thus we are not able to identify with it.

By not reacting to anger we do not reinforce it; it then burns out and dies away. We say that it burns by the flame of awareness and seeing: understanding. The other way of dealing with anger, which may seem more difficult, but which sometimes happens naturally, is by the powerful experiencing of love. Indra expressed this kind of love in the story, so that when this love is experienced, anger (the demon) is eliminated from the body and mind.

The next thing was the forked road: confusion, doubt, perplexity, coming to a crossroad. We do not know which to take because there is no sign post; in the outside world we are lucky because there are signs, but on the spiritual path there are none. We have to use our feelings to find the right way. Or, if we get confused we have to sit there with the confusion and work on it gently until we cut through it. We do not try to be clear when we are confused; if we sit with it, it will clear up by itself. When we try to be clear we avoid what is actually happening.

The next thing that came out of the ant-hill was the turtle, or tortoise. The turtle is attachment to existence; to our body and mind; to the five aggregates: body, feeling, perceptions, mental formations, and consciousness. We want to be the way we have always been. This is conditioning, 'Sankhara' in Buddhism. That Sankhara or character structure is so strong on our personality that we cannot escape – we cannot be free. Freedom is liberation from attachment to our aggregates, to body and mind and all these conditions in our consciousness. But we use them – we use *them* instead of being used *by* them. We make use of our perceptions by applying awareness, so that our perceptions become a tool for dealing with the world; using our senses more effectively, we can use our conditioning to function in the outside world. We cannot do our daily work from the void; being is that way, but functioning and becoming is another way. We have to use certain conditions to deal with the world, with people, with circumstances; it is not dishonesty, it's the way things are.

A snake crossing the river doesn't go straight, he cannot, he has to go in a zigzag fashion. That is the way of living in the world; we have to use *upaya*, a word meaning skilful or effective means; in other words, diplomacy. We use diplomacy to deal with life in the world, but at the same time we do not lose touch with reality, with the emptiness. We are not overcome with greed, or hatred, or delusion; we are with clarity and understanding.

After the tortoise, we come to the strainer – the hindrances and obstacles in our spiritual path. Buddha lists five things in the scriptures but you could make a list as long as you like depending on what obstacles you have.

The last thing you come up against in the ant-hill is the serpent, the cobra. The serpent is enlightenment, enlightened wisdom. In this state there is complete clarity, totality of being and alertness. It is very powerful, and therefore can arouse fear in us. Buddha had that fear himself before his enlightenment.

13.

THE FIVE HINDRANCES

The Buddha has formulated five hindrances as the main obstacles to spiritual growth and the freedom of man. He presents us with a challenge, in the midst of our contemporary lives. In order to benefit from these concepts of hindrances, we must look very closely and with full understanding at how we get imprisoned in the essence of each hindrance.

The first hindrance is sensual desire and the drive to gratify the senses. The second is ill-will, negative thinking, connected with anger and hatred. This includes resentment and vengeful thinking. The third is sloth and torpor, familiar to everyone. The last is doubt.

Beginning with the first hindrance, we can ask: How does the desire for sensual gratification hinder spiritual growth? Perhaps it is just a long-standing tradition in Eastern religious practice: to achieve detachment from sensuality. We can best approach an understanding of the meaning of this hindrance by viewing it from an unexpected angle. Let us see it as a hindrance when we associate spiritual development with high goals and rarified states and identify sensual gratification as lowly and inappropriate to spiritual attainment. This mode of thinking can become an obstacle, putting us into conflict with our natural tendencies and attachments. Conflict over desires creates a negative attachment to the senses, and ties us to the sensual world, the empty village.

In all the Buddha's discourses, he admonishes monks to stay clear of sensual distractions. He impressed the monks with the disgusting nature of sensuality in order to keep their full attention on the practice and devotion of the holy life. This was a clever technique on his part for creating single-mindedness of attitude. But it became an obstacle when it was followed blindly, when it was taken literally to mean that sex and sensuality were inherently evil. This idea leads to obsessive patterns of thoughts, all centring on sensual objects and their rejection, and to lack of mental clarity.

When we talk of sensuality, we refer to the five physical senses. When our experiences come through the eyes, ears, nose, mouth and touch and mingle with desire, they become hindrances, rather than passing phenomena. But in the practice of Vipassana, we are taught to not shut off the senses; rather, to be open to every one of them with full attention. In this way, we work through our obstacles by putting ourselves in their world, rather than shutting them out and leaving them like a hidden menace. It would be easier to retire to a forest or a cave, and see nothing but rocks and birds. But living in the world is harder, more exciting, and valuable for learning insight. This is, of course, a matter of personal choice. It puts us in an awkward position to deny the very senses that we rely on for experiencing our lives. Living with an acceptance of them leads to insight about how we are ruled by the need for gratification. We can use our senses to deepen our perception of ourselves and of others, while strengthening our wisdom and watchfulness. In this way, we take sense desire as a challenge, with the possibility of converting an obstacle into a tool. We must learn to enjoy our faculties without being victimized by them. This is why in Vipassana we observe clearly how the sensual desire arises and how much power it holds over our consciousness. Then, too, we can notice if our attachments are weakening, and when we are becoming free. That is the way to use our potential obstacles as tools. It is a

more effective technique than suppression, which only sub-
merges the effect. If something is not dealt with, it will emerge
at some later point with explosive energy behind it. We can see
the effect of this in people who have been politically oppressed,
or sexually oppressed, exploding into violence and aggression.

Allowing sensual pleasure to become an available object of
awareness leads us to insight into how compulsive we are in
relation to it. The best attitude to develop is freedom in
relation to desire, sex and sensuality. In other words, having
the freedom to act out needs without being compelled to do so
– freedom of choice. Sometimes, when people become
involved with one another, they fixate on their sexual relationship and forget to attend to the work they need to accomplish.
This can become compulsive behaviour in an effort to avoid
losing a pleasurable experience. Even in meditation practice,
we can struggle to achieve pleasant states of mind and then
become addicted to maintaining them, or recovering them.
The mind is always restless, and compulsion is a manifestation
of restlessness.

Not only blissful states of mind and body but overwhelming
states of consciousness can become obstacles. We might cling
to the experience of being overwhelmed, without proceeding
further in the process. Perhaps, when we release strong body
blocks, we experience a surge of sexual energy. In this case,
rather than becoming fixated on the feeling, we can 'marry
ourselves', accepting being in the momentum of the energy,
arriving at a centred place in that energy to proceed onwards in
our work. It is important to distinguish between sexual *energy*
and sexual *desire*, or lust. Desire arises from the mind; it is
thinking without necessarily any biological needs being
expressed. This could be an instance of simply reaching out
for pleasure and distracting entertainment. By simply looking
at this process as it arises, we achieve a simple attitude in
relation to it, and hence quietness of mind.

There is no reason to obstruct sexual energy, or feel guilty if
it arises in our practice. It is an understandable experience at
the human level of reality. Most people, in fact, are not
familiar with this energy. Often, they experience sexual
frustration, arising from not being able to feel because of too

much blockage in the body. This becomes a problem of rigidity. Rigidity operates on both the physical and mental levels. When sexual energy is blocked, the personality is blocked. Then the mind becomes rigid with rules, manners, and fixed modes of communication. Physically, we become controlled and restricted. This presents dangers to the well-being of our physical system. Even high meditative states will not help if this rigidity is not broken through.

The tendency in such a situation is to become cut off from the world and to confine ourselves to a narrower and narrower reality in which we feel safe from threat. We experience conflict because of our need to come out and relate to others. This is prevented by our small self, tied into rules and restrictions, like a frog living in a small pond who has never experienced the ocean. This conflict arises in the midst of our biological urge to connect and relate; it pushes and pulls at us, creating distortions of free-flowing energy. In this state, we experience no freedom.

Rigidity also includes attitudes of stubborness, irritation, and annoyance. It signifies a lack of free-flowing energy leading to tight reactive responses. When this energy can flow freely, it unifies and softens one's relationship to oneself and everything around. It can lead to a completely expansive state of loving energy, without interfering in others' space or being in disharmony with whatever may be around. Sometimes when the energy is released, its power causes the body to shake; especially if it is energy that has been blocked at the sexual level. When this happens, it is important to be open to this pelvic expression without a striving attitude. Striving is connected, again, with sensual desire, the longing to experience. Instead, we can look at the experience in the moment, without anticipating future needs. In this way, any state of experience becomes an object of awareness rather than a dilemma. This is the open path of seeing through applying intelligence.

The second hindrance is ill-will. This is a deeply rooted trait, sometimes called a sleeping dog, because only when it is aroused does one notice it, and then it jumps up and bites. It is the kind of attribute that needs stimulation to bring it to the surface. In pleasant states of consciousness, it hides; but with arousal, anger, discomfort and frustration will manifest themselves. Ill-will is the deepest manifestation of this attribute, leading to hatred, like the root of a tree pushes to the surface. When anger is suppressed, we experience resentment, a manifestation of avoidance. Resentment is a result of holding on to feelings which we do not feel free to acknowledge or express. In this case, we are held back by some image, or idea, of what is proper, and some desire to be seen as good. This leads in turn to irritability and short temper, and an increasing need to avoid situations that will arouse the suppressed feelings. The standard of peacefulness has become an obstacle, hiding a deeper layer of intense agitation. This includes the attempt to achieve tranquil states of mind through chanting and other meditative techniques. Avoidance and non-acceptance of negativity is the root of the second hindrance.

We can see through this process of understanding ill-will, and the negative states associated with this hindrance, how it obstructs spiritual growth through creating suppression, loss of energy, and despair. In Vipassana, the object is to uncover this process by looking at every level of manifestation of this hindrance, and to its point of arising. We can see how a feeling or idea came about by uncovering every detail of its arising. Penetrating in this way leads to the dissolution of the feeling at its core. This is a natural process of clearing rather than a plan arising from ego's image and intentions.

The third hindrance is sloth and torpor, a theme familiar to all of us. Physical sleep is a common sign of just being fatigued and is readily relieved compared to mental lethargy and dullness, the fetters of mental sleepiness. This sensation arises from encountering the difficult, and wanting to avoid going through a full experiencing of it by escaping into drowsiness and mental inactivity. Then the mind becomes slackened and weak, sluggish rather then pursuing the work of meditation. This can become a very dreamy state, dull and heavy, without focus or attention, a meandering mind. Focusing on this dullness, with extended attention, while sitting through this state will produce more energy, burning away the dullness.

The longer and deeper we allow the process of looking and sitting to penetrate our dullness the more energy is produced. Then the obstacles are eradicated. This is no excuse to stop.

Whether dullness leaves completely, or uncovers more resistance, discouragement or slackening off of effort is simply further slothfulness. We cannot rest on achievement. We can progress only by carrying on with perseverance and patience. Staying fully open and alert to energy, we will experience its pouring forth into our process, providing strength and clarity. With full attention there comes a strong vibratory energy at the centre of awareness, unifying the field of consciousness. In that state, nothing matters, although we are still hearing, seeing, tasting. The body adjusts to the natural posture for its well being, and we are free of agitation and restlessness. That is when peacefulness comes. All this comes about without intention or wilful pushing, but with loving attention and easefulness. For a time, we are free of dullness.

The fourth hindrance is worry and anxiety. This hindrance arises from unhappiness deep within the mind. We might express it as turmoil, frustration and paranoia in the psychic world. We become restless, easily distracted, and always looking for diversions. We move endlessly from thing to thing, object to object, pointlessly. Being dominated by this hindrance is like being dust scattered by the wind. The movement depends on the force of the wind. We lose concentration and focus, and must yield to the wanderings of the mind. Instead of insisting on another mental state, we can allow this one to remain; we wait and see how long the storm is going to last, and watch ego suffering through it. We just wait with awareness. There will be some urge to take action, to change things. This is a subtle form of the hindrance itself, continuing to manifest restless action out of despair. The task is to continue watching till the storm naturally subsides; and with this change comes renewed energy. Struggling against this natural process will lead to a great waste of energy, and additional waves of restlessness and anxiety. Non-action is the best attitude in this situation. It will not feed the flame of scattered energy. Non-action becomes the most powerful weapon in this case. The Vipassana approach is to allow and to calm things down through awareness, rather than denying or trying to alter the situation.

The last hindrance, doubt, is related to worry, restlessness, and sloth and torpor. Indecisiveness is a characteristic of doubt: we cannot decide whether or not there is such a thing as enlightenment; or, if there is, we are doubtful that we can achieve it. We become tied up in uncertainty and become insecure about continuing to do the work we have started. But at the same time, we are driven toward some goal and are anxious to proceed. So we cannot leave the situation as it is; and we cannot proceed either. We are in conflict. That is doubt. We cannot let it go and we cannot stay with it.

There is nothing to be done in this situation, as with all the other hindrances. Action can only complicate the situation. We must reside in a quiet, watchful space and attend to the noises of doubt and uncertainty, that inner dialogue. Trying to weigh everything and come to a conclusion is not effective since it arises out of the confusion, rather than stillness. Trying to work it out will only increase the doubt. Instead we can watch the doubting game with interest and detachment, until some true feeling arises. When that feeling comes, some clarity will arise and will provide guidance to the next action. It may be a very brief moment; but the impulse will arise from a source of alertness and bring about authentic action, sureness in movement. It is not constant and will subside to doubt once again. Instead of struggling against this sequence, we can settle back and surrender to the reality of change, and benefit from the moments of clear seeing, when all the phenomena of doubt disappear like an illusion.

Hindrances are not be taken as excuses for ceasing to work, or for avoiding the practice. Instead, as described above, they can become *objects of our awareness* as they manifest challenges to our practice and objects to strengthen our focus. They can help bring about wisdom and discovery of capacities and strengths within us. In any case, we have nothing else to work with. We must work creatively with them, accepting their companionship without self-blame; otherwise, we suffer loss of energy and the positive attitudes that help us toward progress on the path.

Everything that arises passes away, like the wind and the rainstorm. The end is in our understanding of any situation *as it is*, rather than the situation itself. Things will constantly arise, since that is the nature of phenomenal reality. We can relate to this fact with an attitude of conservation – conservation of energy. When we find ourselves in the midst of a particular situation, we apply our understanding as a basis from which to be in a helpful relationship towards it. Then we dwell in the realm of freedom; we let things be, without conflict, and accept whatever arises, confident in our attitude of awareness. Then wisdom arises and flows through whatever our particular reality may be, creating a reality of freedom.

14.
MĀRA: OBSTRUCTING FORCE

Let us look into the meaning of Māra. Māra played a very important role in the life of the Buddha. The first time he came across Māra was during his journey away from his parents' home to become an ascetic. He was riding a horse in the dark night when he heard a voice saying, 'Oh, Siddhattha, in seven days' time you will become an emperor. Why run away?'. The Buddha stopped the horse and listened and realized that it was Māra's voice. He acknowledged it and continued on his journey.

The second time the Buddha encountered Māra was when he was meditating under the Bodhi tree just before his enlightenment. There he met Māra in a fearful and difficult situation, but because he acknowledged that Māra was present, he succeeded in going on along his way.

Often in Buddha's life after he had become enlightened, Māra came to persuade him to something bad or to go back to the palace of the king. But because Buddha immediately acknowledged Māra, saying, 'Māra, I know you,' Māra always vanished immediately.

Testing situations continue as long as we have a body and a

mind. Whether we are completely free or not, we have to meet with different testing situations; then we can cope with them more easily. Saying. 'Oh, no, not this again!' means that we do not want to meet the testing situation. We just want to run away from it.

But we cannot run away, for it runs after us. In Buddha-Dharma this is called *karma*. It accompanies a person like a dog running after meat. The dog catches the meat and eats it. We cannot really run away from karma. It always follows us. There is no escape from it. Even if we have power, we cannot escape karma. Karma has to be eaten instead of allowing it to eat us. If we eat karma, then it is digested and its negative energy is destroyed.

As we say in Thailand, 'No Māra, the perfection is not ripe', meaning that if we do good things without difficulty or without a challenge we shall not be able to do them intensively. Difficulty or interference in doing good things or in working on ourselves is considered to be the best thing for strengthening our personality. Māra is the interfering or obstructing force, and so the stronger the Māra, the more perfect we become.

Māra is the opposite of the positive or constructive forces within us, and lives together with these forces. Māra is not an inherently bad thing, but rather something to remind us of the other side of ourselves which we might otherwise forget, and it teaches us to be aware of this opposite side without falling into its trap. With this understanding, we can stand on our own feet, taking situations as opportunities for further development, for learning, for strengthening and for overcoming weaknesses.

Māra can be seen in five categories. The first of these is called the five aggregates of attachment, the group of psycho-physical processes, energies, within us. We are the combination of aggregates. I will mention each of them briefly.

The first aggregate is body, which includes bodily activities, bodily movements, all physical elements, processes and energies within us. The second aggregate is feelings – sensations, not emotions. The third is perceptions. I use the plural because, like feelings, perceptions come through the six senses. The fourth we usually call habit tendencies or impulses – *sankkhara*. This aggregate is mostly concerned with karma, both negative and positive, and karma formations or habit tendencies or impulses. The last aggregate is consciousness. So there are five aggregates in this first category of Māra – one physical and four mental. The Buddha emphasizes the necessity of understanding our aggregates; their needs, their desires, everything involved with them and our relationship with each – body, feelings, perceptions, habit tendencies and consciousness.

If we are not wise in our relationships with them, we can be caught up in any one of the five aggregates and then they become burdens. Some people, for instance, hold on to the body, and are trapped in it. Some people may be fixed upon sensations and feelings, others upon perceptions. Some people get imprisoned in their own karma or habit tendencies, and become dominated by impulses instead of being liberated by their relationships with them. As a consequence, they can be under the influence of consciousness.

That is why in coming to liberation it is the consciousness that is liberated. One becomes consciousness, and then consciousness is free from all karma, positive and negative, boredom, impurities, the destructive and unhealthy things that pour into it through the senses. So the way to work is to flow into the senses with full awareness so that things will be seen as they are. They do not have to be stored up in consciousness because awareness takes care of the processes of filling and emptying out.

We are living with Māra, so we have to know Māra. Sometimes Māra wants attention, and we might experience this in a frightening form or in an unhappy way. We have to learn to communicate with Māra, then there is no trouble. It is our aggregates that are at the manifestation level so that is where we must be in total communication with ourselves.

The second category of Māra is *kilesa*, meaning impurities. All the negative, destructive, unhealthy states are understood by the one word, *kilesa*. These aspects of Māra may become violent and aggressive. They include such states as anger, resentment, envy, greed, hatred and delusion. There are many others. We have to take notice of and understand all these states of *kilesa* instead of being driven by them. We can use them for constructive purposes.

We can learn to use anger to deal with certain situations without getting angry (in the sense of accumulating anger). This is using anger constructively. We may also behave as an angry person because in certain situations this is a useful tool. You may have heard of teachers being violent with pupils, beating and hitting them in order to wake them up. In Zen stories students sometimes become awakened or gain *satori* because of being kicked. Some people cannot wake up easily because their sleep is so deep, and then the Teacher must use some kind of conscious shock to rouse them.

Instead of accumulating *kilesa*, we use it for constructive purposes. When we become completely liberated we know when and how to use it. It does not destroy us and it does not harm others. Then our being appears like a lotus leaf. We are free in our relationship with *kilesa* and these states then have no power to dominate or direct our lives. We can see them, but we do not have to entertain them. We do not have to do anything with them, only see them for what they are.

True knowledge or insight is power. At the moment you are dominated by a *kilesa* and you know immediately, at that point you become free. Then you can stay with yourself. The problem is that we usually do not recognize *kilesa* soon enough. Māra has the characteristic of always trying to find a way to dominate and delude you, to distort your perceptions, your thoughts and views and to distort your consciousness. So if we are truly aware every moment, *kilesa* is not given a chance. This comes naturally when we achieve liberation. Constant awareness becomes one's life.

We do not have to try to destroy *kilesa* permanently. We say that we destroy it only in the sense of being separated and liberated from it. It has no meaning and no power over us as long as we know it. So we destroy the compulsion of *kilesa*. We break our contract with *kilesa* and then we can relate freely with it without obligation. If we feel a compulsive urge to destroy all impurities, we are only suppressing *kilesa*. Then we would become violent later on, and in that moment we lose awareness and understanding.

The third category of Māra is *abhisankhara*, the powerful

conditioning. This includes moral and immoral activities. It also includes activities higher than moral action, such as attachment to spiritual attainments.

Moral activity is Māra in the sense that we hold on to our good actions or to the *idea* of being good, becoming better or more advanced. Thus we become moral on the surface and then look down on others who we consider to be immoral. If there is clinging to the idea of doing good, then one becomes frustrated in seeing bad things happening, and there is no true integration of the whole of one's being. This is Māra. In the East, people typically do good things to gain merit, but in accumulating merit they are actually accumulating Māra.

The second aspect of *abhisankhara* is demerit: doing bad things, making mistakes, doing wrong. When we do wrong things or make mistakes we usually blame ourselves. We say that we do not want to continue on a negative path; but still, deep down at the unconscious level, we are holding on to it, wanting to behave in this way, wanting to make ourselves suffer more to deepen our conditioning, deepen our sleep. We want to wake up, but at this deeper level we want to sleep. People often feel that if they do not have suffering and problems they do not exist. They feel that they need their negativity in order to communicate with others.

In Thailand the story is told of a dog who had a wound in his head which was painful and full of worms. The dog couldn't be happy anywhere – lying down, sitting, resting. He couldn't be happy because of the pain. At one point he realized, 'Oh, I cannot be happy because of the wound in my head.' Then he stopped running and started looking. He let his wound be cured and then he was free from unhappiness.

This story applies to our situation. If we run for comfort, run after groups, meeting this guru and that guru and so on, without realizing what we are doing, what the real issue in life is, then we perpetuate our suffering. We do not look into the real issue but instead want comfort from outside ourselves. This holding on to and grasping after externals is an activity which avoids looking at what is really happening; it does not make use of our intelligence. We think that we do not have happiness because of suffering, or frustration, or confusion.

This is the voice of Māra. Māra becomes happy if she can delude us in this way.

The third aspect of *abhisankhara* is something higher than moral or immoral activities in life. It pertains to attachment to spiritual attainments. Higher states of consciousness, and all kinds of mystical, spiritual and religious experiences belong to this category of Māra. An example of this in Buddhist terms is the attachment to achieving different stages of *jhana*, meditative absorptions in form and formlessness. These states are still in the realm of Māra if we are not free from our experiences, good and bad. We say that all experiences must be transcended. When we cling to experiences, then we are afraid of losing them. This attachment is *ilesa*. Māra is supporting her own activities in this way, but we are not aware of Māra. Without attachment to experience we do not carry any experience with us; we just travel freely.

This does not mean that we must not have experiences; but your experiences will become wider if you do not hold on to them: you are then open to other experiences.

The fourth category of Māra is concerned with deities. The idea of deities comes to many people when they meditate. They want to communicate with deities, but in so doing they are living in the world of Māra again. The Pali term for this realm of deities is *deva*. We are *deva* too when we come to radiance or shining being. I prefer to refer to these shining qualities as within – not out there. Some shining qualities like to dance, some like to smile, some like to sing.

All symbols of religion, which are symbols of deities, are the expression of our own shining qualities. It is easier for people to see these qualities in pictures and symbols, because they cannot see them in themselves easily. We have to understand that these symbols are reflections of our qualities only. When we see deities, we can look into ourselves. It is as though we were looking into a mirror. So deities become Māra when they keep us with them, keep us dependent on them. We depend on the deities to feel good, and the deities depend on us in order to entertain us. So no one is free.

The last category of Māra is death. Death is Māra. We refer to death as the non-functioning of physical activities or the cessation of physical functioning. Death becomes the thing that stops our development and cuts off our chances for further development. Death also becomes a condition of wandering around in *samsara*. Death will keep us in *samsara*. It does not want us to be free.

Death inside, meaning feeling dead inside, feeling lifeless and unproductive, is also cutting ourselves off from development. We become negative about life because Māra creates problems and difficulties, and obstructs the flow of life. This feeling of deadness can be useful if you can *look at it* and *go into it*, taking Māra for an object of meditation. Then you will become clear about feeling dead; Māra vanishes; you are alive, and can move on.

From all these categories we can see that Māra is always involved with our lives. She is not really something outside ourselves. There is a connection between what goes on inside us and what goes on outside. So people have their own Māra which is connected with the outside world of Māra.

Māra exists in three planes of life. The first plane is called *kama*, the world of pleasure. Pleasure can be both healthy and dangerous to life if we do not understand it. If we understand pleasure, we can have pleasure in a liberated way instead of being caught up in it, thinking it is an end, the only thing in life – falling into the trick of Māra. This does not mean that we should not use Māra or that we should not experience pleasure. We should understand the meaning of pleasure, and thus be free in relation to it. It is ruthless to think that we must not have pleasure, or that we must cultivate asceticism. We are so hard on ourselves in this way. On the other hand, if we think that we must have pleasure only, then we veer to the other extreme.

The second plane of life is the plane of form, referring to both material and spiritual forms of experience – beautiful forms, beautiful shapes, beautiful experiences. Coming to this plane of life people become *devas*; they become radiant, shining, purer, cleaner and clearer. This plane emphasizes form as essential. The artist thinks the form of something is important, like the dance. In the spiritual realm we come to the form of the meditative experience and we apprehend certain states. They all are beautiful. They are all good and healthy.

The third plane is the formless plane. This refers to spiritual experiences – experiencing the infinity of space, its formlessness, its emptiness. Experiencing the infinity of consciousness, seeing consciousness has no form, brings us to a state of nothingness. We cannot say whether it is space or consciousness. This state is called no-thingness because it has no form. Even space does not seem to exist and consciousness does not seem to exist either – just no-thingness. The last state of this formless plane is a very subtle perception which is a state of neither perception nor non-perception.

These are the planes of life in which Māra still operates. So we live in Māra in these planes. We can understand Māra. This does not mean that we destroy Māra. It means that we can be free from Māra while we are still with her.

It is interesting to see that in this analysis there are three planes of existence and four levels of consciousness. The first level is connected with the first plane; the second level with the second plane; the third level with the third plane. The fourth level of consciousness, which is called the enlightened or liberated consciousness, does not have a plane.

We say that liberation is everywhere, on any plane. The liberated person can live on any plane of life. He has freedom to live, to be here or there on any plane. There is choice when there is liberation. So there is no fixed plane for the liberated consciousness, the liberated person.

The Buddha did not analyze or assign a definite plane to liberation. In fact, he said nothing about it. We can see the reason. If there were a fixed plane for liberated consciousness it would be seen as a division and something outside ourselves. But in fact it is everywhere, on every plane, so we need not strive for a plane of existence or cling to the hope of being in a certain place. We can strive only to be free and then we can live in any plane of life that we want. With freedom, we have clear movement and choice.

So the idea of liberation is clearly connected with purifying or developing our consciousness. In other words, we say consciousness is in a figurative sense the carrier of karma. It will not have the power to dominate when it becomes scattered. If we can break the force of our karmic energy, then there is no longer any compulsion, and freedom results. Consciousness is then liberated, and no longer carries karma.

Consciousness is everywhere in our bodies, in our feelings, in our perceptions, in our *sankhara* (mental activities). The body has consciousness in every cell. In the realm of the mind, consciousness is there too. So if we are going to get to the heart of consciousness, as it were, we have to go through our bodies, our feelings, our minds, our thoughts and our ideas. Every time we do this, we are purifying and cleaning them and developing the positive side of these parts of ourselves.

When consciousness is liberated, it is free in its relationship to Māra. One can be one's self, while still living in this world of Māra. Māra provides the world. Even Buddha was living in this world of Māra, as a human being.

You can conclude for yourself what Māra is. It should be clear that it is neither good nor bad, but contains properties of both. It is something we have to be free from while still living with it. If you try to get rid of Māra, you will not be able to live with it in harmony.

Love flows with freedom. Love is the link; we cannot be separate, we cannot be divided. With love we are always together, even if physically separated. When we come to liberation, the feeling of being together will come to us. That is the manifestation of life. We feel separate because of delusion. When you are free from all the ideas which separate you, then you are integrated; love and understanding, or wisdom, flow together. It is not far, but is something too close to us to see.

The liberated person has choice. He can live in the formless plane or in the plane of form. A liberated person can also choose to live in the plane of pleasure. The choice is made freely and his purity is maintained.

Then life becomes much richer, without clinging to richness. The important thing is to know Māra – only to know, nothing more.

15.
TWO ASPECTS OF WISDOM: EQUANIMITY AND LOVE

Love is the movement of unity, of oneness, unifying the world and the universe. Everything is one; this unification is love; to unify is love's function. Equanimity creates but at the same time transcends duality. Equanimity recognizes good and bad, body and mind, in fact all dualistic concepts; at the same time it stands above duality, so that it does not get caught up in the concept of duality. Love and equanimity become the two sides of wisdom; wisdom-love and wisdom-equanimity.

Equanimity is the translation of the Pali term *upekkha*. Literally, *upekkha* means gazing, or approaching things with attentiveness. Literally, it is a form of meditation. It comes into many categories in Buddhism, because of the different aspects of life. *Upekkha*, or equanimity, is realized through feeling. We have three forms of feeling: pleasant, unpleasant and neither pleasant nor unpleasant. The third category is *upekkha*. *Uphekkha* is feeling neutral, neither agreeable nor disagreeable. For ordinary people, this kind of feeling is sometimes connected with understanding, sometimes with not understanding. Sometimes, if it is separate from understanding or wisdom, it may lead to an extreme form of equanimity – indifference, which is a negative form of detachment that can lead to apathy. Usually, however, equanimity is connected with wisdom or understanding. It applies to people who are on the path.

Equanimity functions in the social aspect of our lives, becoming the virtue of the ruler, the leader, or the parent. Parents should show equanimity towards their children. There are two meanings: first is the rectitude of action, taking the right unprejudiced action. The second involves not taking sides, becoming a mediator, a negotiator, making the right judgement without being biased by philosophy, or by groups of people, or by partners. This is the great quality of kingship. In the East, the king plays a very active role in society. Thus, a frequently occurring word in Buddhist literature is *dhammaraja*, the righteous king, which is similar to Plato's concept of the philosopher-king. The ruler of the country must be a person who knows, not just in an intellectual way, but intuitively, who knows with the *heart*.

Equanimity is essential in family life, too. You can see how you practice *upekkha* toward your children when something happens to them – whether you take sides with this one or that one, or whether you remain neutral, listening to both parties, and trying to make the right judgement. *Upekkha* is a very important social virtue. You can see that in the political world, if people practised *upekkha* the world would be a better place.

The third way of equanimity is a form of meditation called *jhana*, or meditative absorption. In tranquillity meditation, meditators are supposed to achieve different stages of *jhana*. In the third stage of *jhana*, or meditative absorption, equanimity begins to arise. In the fourth stage equanimity is balanced with awareness. When attaining the fourth stage, attentive awareness arises in the meditator. If the meditator is not locked in the experience of meditative absorption, but is open to new things coming up, then attentive awareness comes into being to balance equanimity. If equanimity is too strong in that stage, a person can become passive and spiritually neurotic. But equanimity itself is healthy, because it is moral; it is the moral, healthy state of consciousness. Correct proportion is important. We have to find the middle path, or the balanced state. Thus, equanimity in *jhana* is actually morality, or the moral state of consciousness, the virtue that helps the meditator transcend bliss and joy and suffering. Both sides of experience, the happy and the unhappy sides, are transcended by coming to this equanimity. At the fourth stage of *jhana* both suffering and happiness are transcended, but it takes a long time to go through the jhanic states; in Vipassana we move in a different direction.

Thus, equanimity is an aspect of enlightenment. The first aspect is awareness, the second is investigation into truth, the third is joy, the fourth is energy, the fifth tranquillity, the sixth *samadhi* or inner stability or unification of consciousness; and the last is equanimity. Within these seven factors of enlightenment, there are two groups. One group is active, the other group is passive. The active group consists of investigation of truth and joy and energy; the passive group of tranquillity, *samadhi*, and equanimity. Now we can see in the state of enlightenment there is a balance, a harmony between the active and the passive. Awareness is the only key to balancing the two sides of enlightenment.

Equanimity, then, is one of the factors of enlightenment, and is a state of mind associated with *samadhi. Samadhi* is a clear, unified, undisturbed, undistracted state of consciousness. Equanimity is another state, but the two are associated and can become one. Equanimity is unbroken attentiveness, unbroken looking or gazing, gazing consistently, but effortlessly; it is the flow of looking without *trying* to look, or without trying to see anything in particular. This is the characteristic of equanimity. You see things for what they are. Whether they are bad or good things, they are all regarded equally. There is no feeling of one thing being more important than another. There is no importance or unimportance attached to what you see. *Upekkha* is one of the essential factors of enlightenment, regarding everything equally, not attaching importance or unimportance to anything. Things are seen as they are, and then they pass away. This is the quality of transcending, transcending what is seen and the seer himself. The object seen does not become important to the mind, and the subject dissolves into the object. There is no self-importance, there is no subjective opinion put on the things seen or heard or experienced. This is an important attitude of life; to be able to see unpleasant things and yet stand above them. If you cannot transcend unpleasant experiences, then you are caught up in what is unpleasant. We have to recognize that the reactive process will still continue because it is a part of the personality and the personality still exists. But now you become the master, you have the key.

This is why you have to develop equanimity, transcending negative states and the reactive process. That act of transcending is the action of wisdom with the quality of equanimity. You have to understand it clearly, otherwise you keep nourishing your negative states. You clean the floor and you expect that there should be no dirt or dust anymore. But eventually the wind blows something in and the floor becomes dirty once more. You have to keep cleaning again and again. In this sense you have to be aware of what you have done. Once things have been cleared up, there is purity; but this can be tainted again because of the senses. We all have senses with which we communicate with the world, and when we communicate there is the possibility of becoming impure. But do not cut off all your senses and become numb, completely paralyzed. You have to remain very alive, and when you are alive you have to use your senses. Using your senses is both useful and dangerous, but you recognize the danger, and know how to deal with it. You are prepared to meet anything; you have antidotes for all possible poisons; you have a doorkeeper who can check everything coming and going through your senses. Being alert, watchful, of what is coming in and going out, even in sleep, the doorkeeper can tell you what comes to you, how to meet your monsters, or how to deal with something frightening or something exciting in your dreams. You can learn to know what is happening in your life both in the waking and the dreaming states, through your doorkeeper.

When you know how to remove impurity, you do it with patience. These processes we are going through are hard because of all the impurities and disturbing influences that have been deeply rooted in our systems, our bodies and minds, over a long period of time. So the process will take time. That is why we find it difficult to work through. But once you have freed yourself of all these things, you feel within yourself clear, clean, pure. If you feel something impure, something poisonous coming to you, and then you sit and really get in touch with it, at the physical level, at the feeling level; it then just melts away. Thus we learn to accept states of being without feeling upset by the return of old patterns. As long as equanimity and wisdom operate you can accept and transcend them. Particularly when you come to certain testing experiences, let things come, see how strong you are, and how aware you are. It is good to be tested occasionally, to remind us what our touchstone of reality is. If you have a touchstone of reality, you see it and prove it to yourself all the time, every moment. You prove your method, your practice to yourself. The more we leave the old patterns alone, the more we actualize the new realizations we have. We reach new insights and new freedoms. We make use of these more and more. Then these things become stronger and stronger and flow through our life. They become part of life, allowing us to outgrow the old patterns so that they eventually die away.

Feeling liberated and seeing clearly allow you to gain insight into duality. You see the physical and mental processes, the relationship between subject and object, but you do not identify with either one of them. You are separate. When you feel separate from duality then you become something else. You feel like yourself, but you also feel like a new person. You feel more and more separate from conditioning and dualistic thinking. You still discriminate, but you do it purposefully.

The danger lies in becoming fixed with equanimity. Once in this state you still have to move on, to mobilize, to move on to more clarity, to more liberation. That happens only if we are aware enough not to get attached to equanimity. This happened to Ananda, the closest disciple of the Buddha. Everybody around him was talking about attainment of equanimity in different stages, and describing it as something very beautiful, a peak experience. Ananda thought that this equanimity was the goal everyone should strive for, but the Buddha warned against this, saying that we must be free from equanimity also. We must not become attached, but learn to let go. We might take a rest somewhere, but we know that it is only a rest on a long journey.

The second aspect of wisdom is love. We have seen equanimity as one side of wisdom that has the characteristics of accepting and transcending. Love is another side of wisdom that has the characteristic of unifying, being one, being in complete integration and union. Love denies all discriminations, all distinctions. In love there is only oneness, oneness of being. When love flows with wisdom, it is the same as equanimity flowing with wisdom. Both sides of wisdom are essential for dealing with the world, and for taking the inner journey through life. Love reminds us of being in oneness, of being together. With love we transcend our discriminations. Wisdom, with love, keeps things together, maintaining the unity of the world, the unity of life, and keeping a unity of consciousness. Unity of consciousness harmonizes and integrates every part of our body and mind and upholds every individual in a relationship. There are three ways of expressing love: through action, physical union, or by words. Love involves people criticizing each other in a constructive way. This is the action of love flowing out. You have to be aware. With love you give, and in giving, you receive. You do not think about taking. The more you give love, the more love and loving energy you receive. Do not feel that when you give love to other people your love will diminish. That is attachment. Love can never die, it is immortal. Like water, which can become ice, or steam, or liquid, love can change form, but it never dies. Love is the same, it flows, in our minds, in our bodies, in our feelings. The action of love is giving, becoming generous, becoming a hospitable host who would not think of taking anything in return. Love flows to the poor, the rich, the needy, to different categories, without discrimination. That is why love unites the world, and pulls it together. That is why love always goes with wisdom.

Sometimes, however, love can become excessive; it is then associated with feelings, or with what we call emotions. It then becomes limited. As human beings are subject to limitations, so our love is sometimes limited – to our family, our closest friends, to the group of people with whom we are familiar. But love flows with relationships, and the more we expand our relationships with people, the more we are open to different people in the world, to different categories of people, to different groups. We should not confine ourselves to a limited world. Even if we have a base, this base will be a kind of vehicle, a tool, by which we communicate with many others beyond it. With this expansion of relationships love can flow out endlessly. When there is no love, it is because we are caught up in some kind of anger, or resentment, or dislike, some kind of irritation, some kind of negative feeling, some attachment. We get stuck. The flow of love is obstructed and you need to let go. Then you realize your anger. You see anger. What is good about holding on to anger? It is simply the habit of your ego, keeping you confined, not letting you flow. When you realize that, anger goes. Sometimes there is anger because of some misunderstanding or because of a strong desire to possess something or someone. This will obstruct the flow of love. The point is not to try to do anything with love. Love is the natural flow of being. The thing is to take care of what comes in to obstruct the flow. That is our task. Pay more attention to that. When you love there is no negativity, no anger, no resentment. Obstruction is our creation. Therefore, we can stop our creation by not creating it. You have to look deeper into habit, or conditioning, to enable you to see that the more you let out your anger, your negative states, the more the feeling of love comes to you. You feel the flow of love in yourself, wherever you are, whoever you are with; and you come into contact with loving energy. Have no doubts: just be open to love and let it flow.

In Vipassana, we acknowledge two structures in meditation. One structure is control, having rules, having power, observing discipline, being attached to tradition and establishment. The second is freedom. Freedom is the structure of Vipassana. Vipassana starts with the freedom to look, to see, to experience and to allow yourself to go through different things, to build up your own way of being and becoming. When you allow yourself to look, you look at whatever arises, pleasurable or unpleasurable. Then surely you face your own conditioning of not wanting to look, not wanting to see. The ego, particularly, does not want to break conditioning; but when conditioning is broken through, freedom and wisdom flow together. The world of the wise is freedom. The world of the man of wisdom is freedom, and freedom and love flow together.

The other side of wisdom is equanimity. Equanimity brings about the attitude of allowing ourselves to *be* in any situation, and be willing to look and go through all difficulties. Equanimity as a state of mind is a kind of poise or equilibrium and evenmindedness. In that state of mind you cannot be distracted, you cannot be disturbed, you can never be upset, because you see things clearly for what they are. The state of equanimity has the power to meet with anything, desirable or undesirable. With equanimity you cannot get carried away. In a sense you are separate, completely separate from phenomena, from what arises. This is the point of not identifying. There is no identification; you become *just looking, just watching, just experiencing*, instead of experiencer or observer. We achieve identity without image. Surely, as human beings, we need the feeling of being something; but that feeling of being something does not have an accompanying image. An image comes with concepts, ideas: feeling goes with the heart. When you feel, you do not care for words or for categories, because you are experiencing what is really happening.

The two sides of wisdom carry us through life. They help us to function as human beings. The Buddha said that love is the maintenance of the world. The world does not only mean the physical world, but each individual. There are many worlds, and there is one world. This is the fundamental issue of love: being in the one world, being in the same boat. We extend our love to people who are still dominated by hate, anger, resentment, hostility, discrimination, conflict. They are dominated because of a lack of love, which means a lack of understanding.

Love flows from us. First, we have to feel the flow of love, then we can see love flowing in our relationship with people, with the world. When you *have* more love, then you can *give* more. When you do not have love you become miserly. There is a lack of generosity. The lack of generosity means that you have so much to deal with inside, which you hold in so tightly that you cannot give. Where there is no feeling of giving, there is no sense of generosity. But when this circle is broken you will see that you can really give: you are available.

see that you can really give: you are available.

16.
ASPECTS OF NIRVANA

Most people have heard about the Buddhist ultimate reality, Nirvana. There is some misunderstanding, however, not only among non-Buddhists but also among the Buddhists themselves, as to what Nirvana is. It is thought of as a state beyond the reach of the common man, reserved only for those who renounce the world. But Nirvana is not something that takes us away from the world – it simply liberates us from the world. It is like a lotus standing above the water, but still existing in the water. We may ask, liberated from what? Liberated from family ties? From inequality? Very few would think of being liberated from the grip of self; but as long as there is no liberation from our false identity, there is no real freedom. We may have a degree of licence, but we are still enslaved to desires and ideas; we are not free.

The truth of Nirvana as discovered and experienced by the Buddha is comprehensible in this life; it is something immediate, right now, not the past nor the future. Yet we always miss the now, that which is close to us, in the same way that we cannot see our own face. We miss the present because of the habit of being with the past or the future; the habit is so

strong that we do not see reality *right now*. Is is possible to
become completely aware without being broken or carried
away? If we can, there is the possibility of seeing what Nirvana
is, because it is visible. The Buddha never used the words
'achieve' or 'attain'; he always said that is is visible or seen by
the wise; it is a subjective personal experience that is paradox-
ically objective because the experience is free from ego, from
that 'somebody' behind the experience, from the experiencer
himself. If it is visible, why don't we see it? What is it? We are
looking for a definition in order to see what Nirvana is; but
that way we will not see it because we are using the intellect to
recognize Nirvana, according to our input: we use the wrong
means and so we come to the wrong end. Nirvana is leading
onwards, lifting you up, making you move on, not allowing
you to get stuck. When we are liberated we can move on; there
is a constant flow of being and becoming at the same time.

It is essential to look into certain aspects of Nirvana that can
be applied to our lives. Nirvana, literally means blowing out
the fires, so that we are not burnt by the fires of illusion, the
world of *Māya*. Usually fires refer to three main impurities;
desire, hate and delusion. We are burnt by desire, hate and
delusion. The last is very subtle; it is difficult to recognize
because we know; because we have knowledge or information
we deny that we have delusion or ignorance. We *think* we know.

Freedom from desire, hate and delusion is Nirvana. It
sounds difficult for us to be free from desire. I explain being
free from desire as being free from the compulsion of desire.
We can transform desire into creative energy for living; it is no
longer desire in the sense that it forces us to do what it
demands. If we have no compulsive desire we can be free; we
can be patient.

As aspect of Nirvana that is not very often talked about is a
wholly developed state of being, *bhāvitattā* in Pali. *Atta* means
'self', not the self as image or impression but self without an
article before it (in another word: *being*). Sometimes it is
translated as 'realization of the self'. I am not happy with the
word 'state' but cannot find a better one. Unless we realize
Nirvana we are not fully developed; we are not in a fully
developed state of being. We talk about mature, fully grown-

up people; we say that when we are children we are not grown up, we are immature, and that when we are adult we are mature. It does not go that way. Many adults are very immature because they are heavily conditioned and shaped by culture, tradition, habits, attitudes; they have very deeply seated characters. Although many people say 'character' is a good thing, it is really the worst thing because it is a fixation and does not allow us to move freely and to use our own intelligence; instead it makes us conform. You will say it is much easier to conform because I already have this character; I simply conform to its pattern. But this makes us very immature, particularly in the spiritual sense.

What is the truly mature person? He is unpredictable – *abhyākata* in Pali. You never know what is going to happen with such a person. In this sense, the mature person is reviewing situations in life every second because of a continuous, unbroken awareness of what is going on within and outside himself. A person who is in constant contact with reality, with the now, is dynamic, flowing freely according to the dynamic process in life. He does not become static or stagnant. He does not have 'character'. The truly mature person has a healthy personality, is free from fear and bondage, is emotionally stable and self-reliant.

The mature person does not get confused. He can let go of anything. There is no holding on, no regret about the past and no speculation about the future. As long as we are anxious about the future and repenting the past, we are immature. We ask: what can we do in our life if we do not have a future? People are afraid of the future; they do not really want to have a future; they want to have everything here, they want to maintain or hold on to what they have now. Fear of losing what they have is also called anxiety about the future. But there is no need to be anxious about the future because the future does not exist apart from our habit of dividing time. The future is the expansion of the now. Why don't we live fully now? We may have a vision of something happening in the future, but our concern is here, now, not in the future. If we are anxious about the future, that is also a concern of the moment. By looking at the anxiety we shall not miss it and shall not allow it to dominate our lives because we can *see* it and therefore *cope* with it. The capacity to deal with what is happening at the moment is required.

In order to be mature we have to make more use of our own human resources. We have a lot to bring out. But where are the resources? Within us. We have to take a journey through ourselves to discover what is within, and what is around us. The journey of discovery is the basis for Vipassana meditation, the way to awakening or enlightenment. Dependence is another characteristic of immature people, whether material, physical, emotional or spiritual. Those who can stand on their own feet and walk freely in the world are mature people. Psychological dependence is slavery. We have to see that we are still in a state of slavery. We can see how we become slaves to ourselves, to our demands, desires, or emotions.

In a way we do not really develop anything, even though we use the term 'the wholly developed state of being'. What we have to do is to see through the barriers, through the world of illusion. We have to see through illusion before we can come to reality. Before we can be free we have to know what prevents us from being free. As soon as we see the barrier, which is the enemy, we will find the capacity and clarity of action to transform environmental support into self-support. We have to take refuge in ourselves, which is the Dharma. We do not take refuge in any other things, but only in the wholeness of being. Nobody can have a monopoly on it; it is freely available. But when we do not see it, is becomes unavailable. We have to use our inner eye – the eye of awareness – to see the availability of what is. Usually we hold on to the idea of being free, without attending to the obstacles standing in the way of freedom. Is it possible to do something with the barrier? When we see the barrier we do not really need anybody to help us; but when we cannot see it, we may need someone's help to point out the path, point out something that we could not see in ourselves.

If we can become completely mature, how can we live in the world? If I have no attachment, how can I have a job, family and friends? If I do not have attachment I shall not have my own identity. In fact, in the process of becoming mature, we are really seeking our *true* identity, which will come into being with another concept, that of no-self or *anattā*, which is the true identity. It is the zero point, no-thing-ness. No-thing-ness is frightening to our false state of existence; but when we actually see it we have no fear. We are free in that state of no-thing-ness, because it is immeasurable, clear and empty, and because it is empty it can be filled with anything, without containing a thing. Anything can come in and go out without getting stuck. We look from there instead of looking from outside, from our false identity. If we look out to the world from inside we can see the world as it is and then we do not get caught up in illusion, but are more and more in touch with reality – emotional reality, or feeling reality, physical sensation reality, the physical world and the world of experiences. When we are caught up in our thoughts and emotions we are cut off communication; then sometimes we feel frightened because we are alone and isolated and not in contact with anything else. But as soon as we open up communication we feel alive; life is rich. We have to use our six senses, five physical and one mental, instead of being used by them, and simply receive their reports.

Difficulties are essential: they test us and deepen our understanding. They provide the situations when we can discover our potentialities. If there are no such situations in life there is no growth, no realization, no maturation. One moment we cry, another moment we laugh or smile; that is life. There is nothing wrong with crying or laughing. They happen when we are in contact with reality. When we know what is happening we do not get lost. If we get lost in crying and laughing then we lose contact; we are overwhelmed by illusion. The world of illusion is created very easily and it stands between us and reality. Illusion takes over when we are not watching our emotions from our centre but from our peripheral selves; we mistake illusion for reality. Reality is then an object, seen as something apart. Operating from the centre, reality sees through unreality, fantasies, daydreams, projections, speculations, and the world of dreams. This world of illusion is like a cloud: we have to use our intelligence and attention to pierce through the clouds so that we will be able to see the blue, clear sky beyond. But if people lose contact with themselves they may find it very difficult to come back; they may rise above the clouds without keeping contact with the zero point, the operative centreless centre.

Nirvana is also described as being in union with something supreme. Arriving at the Nirvanic state one achieves union with what the Indians call Brahma, the wholeness; in Christian terms, we would say being in union with God.

There are similarities in all religions. All the ways point to the same thing. I used to say that if we have trust in a road map we will be able to get to the destination in different ways, because the road map shows different roads leading to the same point. The oneness of experience is put into different categories or languages according to our cultures. If we have to explain things, we do it according to our culture because Nirvana has no language and no words. Our explanation or description of experience is not the experience itself but something about it. It is essential to get into that experience and prove it to ourselves, then we have no doubt. We must never lose contact with the zero point. We return to it, to no-thing-ness and at the same time we are in touch with reality, with illusion, without being caught up in illusion. It is not true that once we realize Nirvana we no longer experience illusion. We still do, but we see illusion for what it is, without any bias. Even after his enlightenment the Buddha was occasionally tempted by Mara – the obstructing force – but he recognized Mara immediately. So long as we have body and mind and personality factors, we are in the world of illusion; but at the same time we are in the world of reality.

The other aspect of Nirvana that is useful to us is concerned with the release of consciousness. Consciousness has to be developed and conditions in consciousness must be trans-cended. We release the negative destructive energies from consciousness so that it can become clear and luminous. The process of cleansing or purification comes through at the point of contact with what is happening, now, at this moment. We have to have continuous awareness, which makes us capable of being in the now. When we are in the now we can clearly see things coming through. If we blot out the now, nothing will come through. We get stuck somewhere in the past or the future. When we open ourselves to the now we are in the creative present and this opens the door to ten thousand things.

The world of illusion is very strong. If we have been living in the world of illusion for a long time it is very difficult to leave it; ego has built up very thick walls, trying to protect itself in that world of illusion. Even if the ego has a glimpse of reality it becomes very frightened. We are dominated by fear and yet we want to be free. If we are not free from fear we cannot live in the now; we are afraid of not gaining what we should gain; we are afraid of losing what we have; we are afraid of wasting our time, doing nothing; we want to be active and productive. When there is no freedom to be, there is anxiety, fear, and guilt; we do not do what we should do, we waste our time doing things which are not worth our while. All these things are experienced in our life, and we wonder whether freedom is possible at all.

The idea of freedom usually refers to freedom from something – from suffering, from fear, from bondage, or from any tie or difficulty. This is the negative aspect of freedom. Very rarely do we think of freedom just in the sense of *being free*, free for being, acting, sitting, listening, talking. This aspect of Nirvana is the freedom of consciousness or the release of consciousness. Consciousness has been imprisoned and must be released.

Consciousness is the core of our personality, the heart of life. It has so many contents, so many states. It can bring us up or put us down, like a ball being kicked here and there. What is consciousness? Animals and plants as well as humans all have consciousness. If you listen to a river you may understand the meaning of life, like the ferryman in the Siddhartha story. Listening can bring about deep wisdom; but we listen very rarely. When we do not listen, we do not understand. We do not even hear what other people say, and so misunderstanding can easily be created in relationships. We block the flow of wisdom. We prefer to listen to famous people rather than to listen to a little child; we do not listen to the movements of the wind; we do not pay attention and are not sensitive to what is going on. When there is freedom, listening becomes a powerful agent it opens the doors to creation.

Consciousness is subject, what we call 'I'. I am consciousness. Without the first person there is no consciousness. But the
first person is always there, being conscious of things inside
and outside. Consciousness has certain conditions and states.
Without a state, consciousness cannot operate. We talk about
lower and higher levels of consciousness. The lower level of
consciousness refers to negative states, being in hell, being
animal-life, being a hungry ghost, being a demon and being
afraid of meeting certain situations. We come down to hell by
experiencing suffering and unpleasant things through our
senses. But hell is temporary, we can go up again to heaven
and down again to hell. This enables us to gain experiences,
both negative and positive, and so builds up our strength. We
can go to heaven through our senses – smelling, tasting,
seeing, hearing, touching – experiencing pleasant things.
There are many levels of heaven and different degrees of
happiness or joy in life. We can travel up through different
levels of heaven. Sometimes we lose ourselves completely in
joy or bliss, and after coming out of this state we find ourselves
down again, feeling very unhappy. These are the vicissitudes
of life that are experienced in our consciousness. Human
beings are somewhere between high and low. They can go up
and down.

In a Buddhist story there is a monk called Mogallana who
had great psychic powers; it was said he could go down and
visit the suffering beings in hell or go up and visit the heavenly
beings so that he could give information to humans about
those beings and how much suffering or happiness they had.
This is the symbol of experience. Any one of us can experience
heaven and hell. Through meditational processes we can
experience heaven, the higher states of consciousness; but
also hell, the lower states, through pain in the body and
heart. All physical, mental, psychological sufferings can be
experienced. Just accepting whatever is experienced means
we are finished with it; but this is very difficult for us to do. We
get imprisoned in the lower states of consciousness because we
find them unpleasant and want to get rid of them; therefore,
we play negative games with ourselves. In the blissful experi-

ences we become attached; we cannot let go of them; if they leave us we become disappointed and depressed; but the fault comes from us, from our expectation and attachment, not from the experiences. If we can let go and are prepared to experience *whatever* happens in our consciousness we do not cause double suffering to ourselves; we neither lose nor gain but just experience and live through.

Gain and loss are the two sides of the same coin; they are only experiences in life. But because of our conditioned opinions on gain and loss we feel unhappy when we feel we are losing something. This is because of holding on, grasping. In a sense we lose ourselves, but we are not even conscious of this loss and do not feel bad about it. But if we lose certain objects we like very much, we feel unhappy because we feel lonely without them. We are afraid of experiencing loneliness. We need to stay with loneliness, sit with it, not go away; see what loneliness says, learn about it, go through it. Without going through suffering and frustration we will never appreciate freedom.

When we are clearly aware of ourselves and of others we see the state of consciousness activating at the moment. Is it something conditioning us, dominating us or directing us to move in a certain way without having freedom? If so, it means that we are prisoners. A prisoner has no freedom. But if we are conscious with clarity and have the capacity to perceive without having to conform to any pattern or condition, our consciousness is free.

We cannot talk about consciousness without talking about states of consciousness. We are completely in the creative present when transformation takes place. If we become completely open to the now, we blot out the past and the future, playing with imagination, intellectual games and ideas. It is very easy to slip back to the past because we are familiar with it. States of consciousness are our culture, our religion, upbringing, education and training.

How can we be free and free ourselves from the conditioned consciousness? Is it possible to be free, to be purely conscious? It must be possible since all enlightened people talk about liberation, awakening, freedom from birth, from aging, from death: that is the state of Nirvana. Sometimes we talk about Nirvana as emptiness. We may not like the idea of being empty but emptiness in this sense is something different from what we imagine it to be. It is the 'abundant void'; it fertilizes life. If we get into such emptiness we come to ourselves, our real being *(attamana)*. In that abundant fertile void there is freedom to look and freedom to be: there is clarity, capacity, possibility and flow; it is not a static state. What we call being is a dynamic movement and is very deep; it always moves gently and deeply; like still water. When this happens there is the possibility of being free. Normally, we look at the world from outside, so we do not see ourselves because the world of illusion is standing in the way: we do not see our real being. It is hidden, as when in watching a movie we see pictures on the screen and concentrate on the moving pictures. We do not see the screen behind them. Freedom of consciousness is like this screen; it is the common ground, 'the delightful stretch of level ground'. If you stretch yourself on the level ground you feel soft, you touch everything fully, you can sense, smell, absorb. That is the real state of being: Nirvana. If we come to our real being we are on this level ground and it is *now*, not the last moment or the next moment; it is right here at this moment. If you can see the possibility of blotting out the past, you will find yourself there. It cannot be produced, but it *is*. That is what we call pure consciousness – the completion of being with ever-expanding intensity.

The process of transcending the states of consciousness is meditation. Meditation is the process for transforming and integrating these states into complete harmony. If you can sit there in your real being – the delightful stretch of level ground – and look out at the world of phenomena and experiences as well as the world of Maya, you enjoy looking; there is inner joy. Joy is not produced; it arises naturally through our pure seeing and perceiving. When we are free of all the conditioned states – Nirvana is also described as the cessation of rebirth – we shall not be reborn because we are born completely. But when we are not born completely we have to be reborn again and again in life. When we are really in the state of being, we do not have to demand anything – everything is there, accessible, available for us to use. Sometimes we wonder what will happen if we achieve this state of Nirvana? Do we become unconscious of the world? Perhaps the world will disappear or we may see the world in a different way. We are familiar with the Zen story of seeing mountains as mountains again. We perceive objects in different ways because of different ways of looking at them. If we look from the pure free whole where there is no conditioning, everything is seen purely, clearly and precisely; there is no distortion, no perversion. When seeing reality we are completely free, even free from explaining it. Because the heart is full we cannot find a word.

But in the process of transforming our consciousness, we have to go through both negative and positive experiences. We have to be prepared to work through, otherwise there is no freedom. Some people may ask, 'Why not find a way that leads us straight to that state without experiencing any suffering?' We always want to find something easy. We want to be given, but nobody can give such a thing to another. We cannot go to such a state without experiencing suffering. Suffering is valuable and essential for developing wisdom and deep insight into life.

By going through suffering we will find that at the moment we come to the release, we are so clear, we feel so wonderful. The Buddha-Dharma emphasizes pain and suffering and people may say that this is a pessimistic outlook; but in fact it is not; it describes the real facts of life. See how we become tied down in life because of conditioned consciousness. We are afraid to break away from any condition, any convention, because we cling to safety and security. If we break away from what we are familiar with, we feel uneasy when we have to assume our roles in the world: we ask, 'How shall I behave if I don't carry all these things with me?' We put our centre of gravity outside ourselves, over there, in other people, in authority figures, when it should be within us. The centre of gravity within us is not the ego, it is self-sufficiency, self-reliance, self-trust. We very often lack trust in ourselves; we always ask for approval, for confirmation, and we cannot take the initiative. See how dependent we are: we all depend on other people in order to feel secure and safe. That is because the centre of gravity is located in the wrong place. If we located it within us we would not find it difficult to take the initiative, to lead life freely. You live your own life. Why be conditioned by other people, by social standards? That is the revolution which is very hard to actualize. There is always the little child within us who is playing the role unconsciously; sometimes we play the role of mother, but this role is that of the little child in early life. In meditation this child is very noisy, demanding this and that, making plans. You may like to see how many plans you make when you sit quietly, and also see whether you can sit quietly without making any programme. When we programme our life we become narrow, deny ourselves freedom.

The worst game we play is the self-torture game. By holding on to certain roles and ideas, we are living up to certain standards, principles, ideas, images; we are torturing ourselves thereby. Many people hold on to their own suffering and frustration and do not want to let it go. We blame ourselves, too; or we blame others; avoidance is the essential part of the self-torture and blaming games. We have to see how often we put ourselves into prison. Sometimes we build up authoritarian images, judging ourselves; we appoint a judge who is sitting in judgement on our life. In psychotherapy the judge is called the 'top dog'; he plays the authoritarian games. The 'under dog' is always submissive or playing the cry-baby game: when you cannot get what you want you cry; when you feel lonely, you cry. There is no end to such games.

We have to understand how we play roles, how we carry this little child within us all through life; we never grow up. We become adults, but we are still little children, particularly at the emotional and psychological level. We are not emotionally stable; we are easily emotionally disturbed and frustrated, when changes take place in life. And yet we want to change ourselves. All these levels of consciousness have to be transformed so that we are purified and return to the common ground – the screen. Yet we acknowledge that all these things exist on the surface, although in a way they harmonize with our personality or our consciousness. First of all, the different levels do not communicate; they do not listen to each other because we have not established the understanding and opened the doors for relationship between the surface and the depth. But there is always a link between the surface and the depth. We are not aware of that link. What is the link between the two?

The link is the interflow of awareness in which there is wisdom and love, so that the surface and the depth are not in conflict; they allow themselves to be as they are; they allow the surface to be the surface and the depth to be the depth. Things come into conflict because of a lack of understanding and communication. Open, honest communication will bring about understanding: it opens the door to negotiation. In life we have to negotiate all the time, so we have to learn to be a genuine negotiator. We have to negotiate with situations, circumstances, with people, so that we recognize and accept them for what they are. Then we can live on good terms. We do not want others to live up to our standards or expectations. They can live their lives and we can live our lives. Then we base our relationships on that openness, honesty and mutual sharing which is love.

INDEX